BASIC BUDGETING PRACTICES

for Librarians

Second Edition

Richard S. Rounds

American Library Association

CHICAGO and LONDON

1994

Managing Editor Kathryn Solt

Cover and text design by Harriett Banner

Composed by Publishing Services, Inc., Bettendorf, Iowa
in New Baskerville and Optima
on Xyvision/Linotype L330

Printed on 50-pound Glatfelter, a pH-neutral stock,
and bound in 10-point C1S cover stock
by Braun-Brumfield, Inc.

The paper used in this publication meets the minimum requirements of American National Standard for Information Sciences—Permanence of Paper for Printed Library Materials, ANSI Z39.48–1984.

Library of Congress Cataloging-in-Publication Data

Rounds, Richard S.
  Basic budgeting practices for librarians / by Richard S. Rounds.—
2nd ed.
    p.   cm.
  Rev. ed. of: Basic budgeting practices for librarians / Margo C.
Trumpeter, Richard S. Rounds. 1985.
  Includes index.
  ISBN 0-8389-0630-3 (alk. paper)
  1. Library finance.   2. Program budgeting.   I. Trumpeter, Margo C.
Basic budgeting practices for librarians.   II. Title.
III. Title: Basic budgeting for librarians.
Z683.R68   1994
025.1'1—dc20   93-47476

Printed in the United States of America.

98 97 96 95 94   5 4 3 2 1

Contents

Figures

Preface

For libraries, and a myriad of other public agencies, money has become increasingly hard to obtain. Competition for funds among these agencies has become more fierce each year, and there is no end in sight. Even substantial increases in taxes do not produce enough for agencies to grow on. Indeed, if one word can describe these times it is "recision."

Recisions are reductions in budgeted funds that libraries, as well as nearly all governmentally related agencies, are requested to make. Often such reductions are a result of stand-still budgets, requiring the budget to be prepared at the same level of funding for the subsequent year as it is for the current year. Since salaries and other operating costs go up from year to year in most situations, the effect of stand-still budgets is to reduce the purchasing power of the budget for the subsequent year. The result then is a recision as the budget is planned. Additionally, it is not infrequent for libraries and others to be requested to make an actual percentage reduction in overall funding for the next year. Such requests then have a double recisionary effect including both the impact of stand-still plus whatever percentage of recision must be used. Also, recisions come with alarming frequency during a budget operational year and thus require replanning and redistribution of fund commitments. These latter recisions are usually required when the parent organization (a school system, municipality or university for example) must reduce its overall expenditures. Such reductions are often the result of tax revenues being received at a less than expected rate or failure to pass some anticipated tax increase through public referendum.

The management of available funds in public agencies has always been an important public trust. However, as funding shortages continue to occur, agency managers are challenged to think differently about how money is utilized. There are no universal answers, but to refuse to accept the challenge to search for answers is to betray the public trust.

This book is designed to help librarians with the task of effective budgeting. When funds were almost always on the increase, additional dollars could be used to meet not only needs, but also wants. But in recision times, the best use of available dollars requires a careful appraisal of every item for which funds are committed. Determining which functions are necessary to the library's survival becomes a more driving issue. This book provides a framework in which the librarian can plan the budget, make critical decisions about funding priorities and carefully manage the funds that are committed to the library budget.

It was necessary to develop a structure through which the various functions, programs, activities and services of the library could be defined and then prioritized in terms of their essentiality to the library framework. These definitions and that structure are found in Chapter 4.

This new edition was devised in order to help librarians deal more effectively with the impact of recisions on the library. Without a rationale and procedure, the library manager, like other middle managers, will take steps that will not lead toward intended goals that should be retained in spite of budget recision obstacles. One of the needs of the library manager has been met through the development of planning processes for the library in *Planning and Role Setting for Libraries* (McClure, et al., 1987). It is now possible to identify differentially in a variety of library situations the roles, goals and objectives of the library. This planning design has the additional strength of interacting with library stakeholders as a part of the process. What has been missing is the necessary relationship of planning to the funds that are committed to achieve the intended outcomes of the planning. The function budget structure and definitions presented in Chapter 4 were developed as a way of achieving this planning and budgeting integration. So while recision budgeting was the initial stimulus in the development of function budgeting, the relationship it fosters with planning becomes an important asset in the process.

This text is designed to be used by students, aspiring administrators or practicing administrators of public and school libraries. It is designed so you can teach yourself or to be used in a classroom setting. Where appropriate, different practice experiences are included for those who are library administrators and for those who are not.

Special thanks are due to Chuck Baldonado, Associate Dean, Library Services, Albuquerque Technical-Vocational Institute. His knowledge of the contemporary library, both in the technical institute setting and in public libraries, has assisted the author with this revision.

J. Harold Washington, Director, Tutorial/Learning Center at the Technical-Vocational Institute Main Campus, has shared unstintingly his knowledge of and skills with PCs and their various contemporary programs.

1
The Budget Cycle

It is July 1 and you are sitting in your office with a few free moments, away from all your duties as a library manager. This day marks the beginning of your fiscal year—the implementation point for your newly approved budget and all the activities you have planned as part of that implementation. You have prepared for this fiscal year throughout most of last year, thinking, planning, evaluating, discussing issues and ideas, setting priorities for the library's program, and replanning what should and could be in your budget. Some of your most exciting dreams are dead, victims of budgetary limitations. You have adjusted your expectations and goals many times, as you discovered the limitations of your parent organization to provide for them, and explored the political climate in which they must be implemented. However, a number of significant goals and their supporting activities are firmly in place, having been hammered out and established through the budgeting process. You have the funds for them and reasonable expectations that they can be carried out. You believe that you have worked through the interpersonal dimensions of the organization to ensure support for these goals and activities.

You feel you have done a good job in preparing for this budget year. You also realize that you soon will begin preparing the budget to be implemented just a year from now. In your mind, you review the process by which budgets are established, that sequence of related parts that produce a budget: studying the needs of the library, evaluating what will keep the library fulfilling its most critical functions, putting the budget together, obtaining funding committments and establishing those management structures that will make it work.

This scenario represents what all budget managers experience every year, and it raises the questions that go to the core of effective budgeting.

Did I understand the budget cycle adequately?

1

Did I work each portion sequentially to the best advantage?

Did I use the previous years' experiences effectively?

Did I get the appropriate inputs from others at the right time?

Do I feel confident of staff and administrative support?

Did I blend the exceptional sources of funding into the budget development effectively?

Did I develop and submit appropriate special-funding proposals?

Were my early projections of revenues supported by the final revenue allocations?

Do I understand better now than I did a year ago, the politics of budgeting within my parent organization?

These and many other questions will occur to you as you ponder the information presented in this text. Although you will need a sense of the entire budgeting cycle, this chapter will present only an overview, with references to other chapters where specific steps are covered. Here we bring all the issues together in a single overview/summary, a kind of map to follow through the budget cycle.

Figure 1 identifies the various parts of the budgeting cycle, and indicates the chapters in the book where those parts are presented. This cycle takes place each year and results in "the budget" that becomes the fiscal basis for the operation of the library for the subsequent year. The development of that actual budget document with the dollars to be expended in its various categories is a part of the cycle, as you will find in the study of this book. It is, however, only a part of a much larger set of issues that both lead to and result from that actual budget document.

You will learn a great deal later about the budget planning processes. Now you will learn about the cycle of activities into which they fit.

BUDGETING CYCLE OVERVIEW

The budgeting cycle is best looked at in reverse, that is, from the end result backward to how that result was achieved. These final products and their specified dates in a calendar year "drive" all the other time lines of the cycle. Usually, the parent organization's final budget is approved within one month before the end of the current fiscal year. Therefore, only eleven months are available beforehand for all of the budget cycle activities. Also, since the library is only one of a number of units in the parent organization's total budget (fire, police, maintenance, academic departments, to cite a few), there must be time for their input before the organization itself seeks final budget approval. Therefore, approval of the library's budget, as a subunit of the parent orga-

Figure 1. Budget Cycle Flow Chart

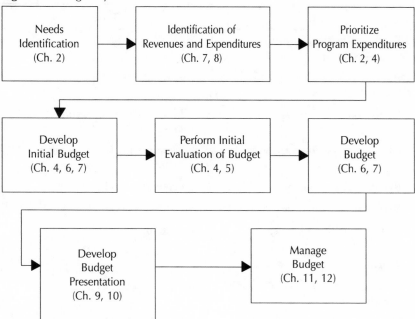

nization (municipality or university for instance), can reasonably be expected from one to four months before the approval of the parent organization's final budget. That interval gives the larger organization's planners time to compile all of the subunit budgets, and thereby devise the total final budget.

Figure 2 shows the steps, in reverse, of the critical elements of the process that leads to approval of the library budget. Each stage comprises distinct activities that are carried out in specific periods of time that overlap to some extent with the activities in other stages. Figure 3 places these elements in the order and usual time frames in which they are carried out during the year.

Let's look briefly at the activities that form the budget cycle. The needs assessment and planning process (discussed in Chapter 2) is the core of the budget, because it involves a study of the library as a set of systems and programs that interrelate and provide the foundation for rational analysis of the budget. It is during needs assessment that patrons and their needs are taken into account. Also during this time, employees and coworkers in the library have a chance to make initial formal inputs into the subsequent year's budget. You are challenged to look critically

Figure 2. Critical Steps in a Library Budget's Approval (in Reverse)

Activity	Time
Budget implementation and management	First day of new fiscal year
Parent organization's final budget approval	Last month of old fiscal year
Library budget approval	1 to 4 months before end of fiscal year
Library budget presentation	2 to 5 months before end of fiscal year
Budget redevelopment	Preceding 2 weeks
Budget presentation development	Preceding 4 weeks
Initial evaluation of budget	Preceding 2 weeks
Prioritizing of program expenditures	Preceding 4 weeks
Identification of revenues and expenditures	Preceding 4 weeks
Needs identification	Preceding 8 weeks

at the entire library function from the "needs" point of view so that you will not (inadvertently) omit anything from your planning.

Needs, as a step in budget development, must be assessed very early in the budget year. As can be seen in the list of activities and dates in figure 3, the ideal is that this activity be carried out by the end of the second month of the fiscal year. In practice (depending on when the library budget is presented), the time frame might extend to the end of the third or the middle of the fourth month. It cannot be pushed much beyond that, or the remainder of the system would be severely compressed. The more time taken by needs assessment (or any other activity), the less time will be available to perform other activities, with the concomitant danger that inadequate time may result in inadequate planning.

The budget will have to be planned and expended regardless of where you are in a library planning or assessment cycle. As the two issues (budgeting and planning) are brought together, you and your library will be in a more powerful situation to communicate your functions to both internal and external stakeholders. "The information that the

Figure 3. Yearly Budget Development Cycle

Activity	Month of Fiscal Year											
	1	2	3	4	5	6	7	8	9	10	11	12
Need ID	—	—	—									
Prioritizing			—	—								
R. & E. ID				—	—							
Develop initial budget					—	—						
Evaluate initial budget						—						
Develop budget		—	—	—	—	—	—					
Develop budget presentation						—	—					
Present budget							—					
Redevelop budget							—	—				
Obtain budget approval									—	—	—	—
Implement budget											—	—
Manage budget											—	—

library uses to describe itself to the larger world tells people what and who the library thinks is important, what the library has done and has tried to do, and for whom. Therefore, the library must build its assessment program to meet the agendas of its stakeholders." (Childers, p. 70). As you may realize, needs assessment and planning is not a solo activity on your part, but a highly interactive information gathering and analysis activity over which you exert control and direction as the library manager. It is one step in the budget cycle where the experiences of the current year and the previous years are brought to bear on predicting and planning the future. Inadequacies in the system, imbalances in expenditure categories, inappropriate personnel deployment, and the need for changes are possible issues for inclusion in needs analysis.

Another important issue in needs assessment is that both formal and informal systems are at work. Input is obtained through formal systems designed to legitimize that input. Such systems include structured meetings, surveys, evaluations of activities, reports, and the like. But informal systems are at work as well, through informal discussions, chance remarks, political observations, information from state and federal government and so forth. Neither system can be considered completely structured or rational; therefore, there is a good deal of sifting to do when you receive input from either source.

Once you have clearly in mind what your needs and priorities are, you have completed the first phase of the cycle. You are now ready to test reality and see what these needs cost and what revenues you might expect to meet them. It is during phase two, covered in Chapter 6–8, that you bring together the pieces of information that define the scope of your potential budget. Obviously, if significant revenues are expected to come to the library through exceptional sources (as described in Chapter 8), you will identify them at this time and include them as part of your budget development and presentation. They may result in reducing your requests for parent organization budget funds.

At this time you want to develop your information as fully as possible, including the maximums in both revenues and potential expenditures. Usually your parent organization will be sending signals about what you might expect in revenues. Ultimately it is that organization (municipality or university administration for example) that will decide what revenues the library will receive for this budget year. But you will decide how that money will be allocated among the needs you identify. Dreaming and scheming often opens up constructive ways to stay within the constrictions of potential revenues. How might personnel be defined and deployed differently? How might automation be augmented to reduce employee costs? Employee time demands? Could additional automation assist in servicing clientele more effectively? How should the library function really be organized for the most effective and efficient performance?

The steps in budget development are:

1. Plan and identify needs
2. Analyze and prioritize activities and services
3. Identify revenues and expenditures
4. Develop initial budget
5. Evaluate initial budget
6. Develop budget
7. Develop budget presentation
8. Present budget
9. Redevelop budget
10. Obtain budget approval
11. Implement budget
12. Manage budget.

Step 3 of figure 1 indicates that you now perform the first stage, prioritizing the potential services. The methods for doing this are covered in some detail in Chapters 3 and 4. Prioritizing is a method of analyzing the potential significance of the various activities you would like to see in the library operation, and your function budget provides the categories for these activities. As you prioritize them, some questions must be answered:

> Which activities are needed for the library to function? These are your top priorities.
>
> Which other activities serve the greatest needs of the groups of library patrons? These are your next priorities.
>
> Which activities or services may be vital to significant political forces in the library community? These must be considered high priorities.
>
> Which activities or services have great public visibility for library patrons? These also would be high priorities.

The real question is how to analyze the importance of the functions, but there is no easy answer for appropriate prioritization. Communities, while sharing a core of expectations for the library, are often different in their interpretations of what this means in practice. Community attitudes and values are important to remember as you proceed. Part of the answer then to the importance of the various library functions, lies in your ability to understand the fiscal/political realities of your parent organization and your community. There are various people from whom you can gain insight into these issues: long-term library employees, decision makers in the parent organization, community library committees, state library personnel. These people should be included in the process, as they can provide important information for you at this time.

However, when it comes to the final prioritization, you alone must make the decisions about the relative merits of the activities or services, and their importance to the directions in which you believe the library should move.

The activities or services listed here are only representative of those that might be identified, as you will find fully defined and explained in Chapter 4. For the moment, accept that these are typical of things libraries do as part of their work, and that money is needed in various support categories (line items) for these to be accomplished. The line items listed along the left hand column of figure 4 are again only representative. Chapter 3 will present the line-item concept in more detail. For instance, money will be needed in the line-item materials and supplies to support the development of the collection. Likewise money must be identified for "personnel" to provide the reserve system of the library.

You are deciding about library functions that, you have concluded, are the most important in your community. You are thereby choosing directions for the library through these decisions. You are creating the kind of organization and services that you consider most productive for the budget year, given all the influences (positive and negative) that you can identify at this time.

TRIAL BUDGET

Now is the time to put the actual budget together in its first-draft form. Additionally, it is at this time that a comparison should be made between the current-year budget and your actual expenditures. In this way, you can begin to compensate in the new budget for shifts in your current operational year. Personnel may have moved from one category of personnel to another; you may have shifted to less print material; or a new academic program may begin to demand different materials/ media. Once the priorities have been set and the resources and expenditures identified, producing the budget may be accomplished by using a sheet similar to figure 4. The functions, programs and activities are listed along side of the chart and the line items along the other. The blanks are completed by transferring the amounts from each activity or service budget sheet for each line item to the appropriate box in the chart. After this the lines and columns are totaled. By adding the totals, first down each line-item column and then across the activity and service totals, you cross-check the totals. The horizontal total and the vertical total should match, if your sums have been accurate for both sets of figures. If they do not, cross-check all the figures against the postings from the activity and service budget sheets. Correct and sum again until they are identical.

Figure 4. Function Budget Recap Sheet

Line Items	Activities or Services				
	Collection	Copy Edit	Liaison	Reserves	Etc.
Personnel					
Employee Benefits					
Materials and Supplies					
Purchased Services					
Etc.					

These totals should be a close approximation of the ones you produced in your expenditure planning (unless you made major changes in your priorities). The result is a "trial budget," which you will evaluate further, which your staff can critique, and which you can share with your informal contacts within the parent organization and your next line supervisor in the parent organization. Your discussion at this point indicates to these persons that this is your first-run, needs-based projection, not your final budget proposal. It is a discussion document, designed to provide a way of responding to identified needs as identified in your planning system. However, you must make it clear that the discussions, which will take place throughout the final approval of the budget, are an expected and needed part of the budgeting process.

The trial budget should be completed not later than the middle of the budget year, to give ample time for evaluation by appropriate people (as well as yourself). When the budget has been totaled for the first time, it may become obvious that additional adjustments have to be made.

The necessity of matching the proposed budget amounts to the projected expenditures and the projected revenues is absolute. When each amount has been summed, you can go back to your revenue projections and make comparisons. The "cut line" established by your maximum revenue projections (in actual dollars) becomes the final cut line of your prioritized list of activities and services. (A "cut line" is the point at which all of your expected revenues have been used up. See figure 23 in Chapter 5.) In making this comparison, you can establish a tentative cut line before you get into your final budget development.

Are the priorities you placed on the services still appropriate? Would further refinements of any of the services release funds to provide for services that now fall below the cut line? Are you satisfied that the funds allocated to the various library functions provide for the best balance in the library programs and activities and services?

McClure has observed with some sensitivity to the frustrations of librarians, "Administrators can either throw up their hands in despair of the current situation, which is an admission that they are not prepared to lead their organizations, or they can take a positive, realistic approach, realize and accept that the halcyon days of funding have passed and accept the opportunity to redesign and retrench in order to do the best possible job under trying circumstances." (McClure, p. 183).

INITIAL EVALUATION

The next step in the budget cycle is a two part initial evaluation: internal and external. The internal phase involves input and evaluation from you and your staff. It can be very helpful , since you know the bottom line of your needs budget and can begin a review of the realities as you perceive them. (This often leads to a closer analysis of your dreams.) Do dreams have higher priorities than some of the activities and services? Are there alternative sources of funding that should be pursued, thereby reducing the local funding total by increasing the total monies in special funding? The internal evaluation helps you deal with the many challenges that will change the needs budget into the final budget you will propose.

The other informal evaluation of the budget that is undertaken at this time is with your contact(s) in the parent organization and your library staff. This person or persons can impart additional realities, for instance, how various items and plans in your needs budget may be viewed by the parent organization in its formal review. This information and these observations are fed back into your internal evaluation and considered as you move toward production of your actual budget.

It is also during this stage that information from the budgets of previous years becomes highly significant. Later, most people who will review the budget will look critically at patterns of expenditures that appear to be greatly different from those of the past few budgets. The more divergent from those budgets your proposal seems to be, the more critical the reviewers will be. It is therefore very important to use this information as suggested in Chapter 9.

	Expenditures 1992	Expenditures 1993	Estimated 1994	Requested 1995
Contract Services	45,669	47,043	49,386	45,292
Capital Outlay	1,826	1,882	2,063	6,157

Contract services are those services that you buy from some person or organization from outside the library, like a lease for the services of a copy machine. Capital outlays are funds spent for the purchase of equipment, like a copy machine. Contract services also can include services provided by a consultant or business, like the development of a program for your PC.

For instance, your discussion with your supervisor has indicated that leases of equipment are being looked at critically by your parent organization. In studying your operation, your copy machine budget seems to be a potential issue. You call your vendor and determine that indeed you could use the same amount of money now being used in leasing to achieve a purchase of your machines in just over two years. While you have some nagging concerns about maintaining state-of-the-art equipment and keeping maintenance costs down, you believe it is politically wise to make this change.

In the figures above you notice that for 1995, $4,094 has been moved from contract services and added to capital outlay to show the effect of the purchase.

Every line item in the budget must be considered with the same care. Apply whatever limits you have informally identified through your sources in the parent organization and identify the trouble spots, then evaluate each of them. Are there alternatives? Are such levels legitimate for library effectiveness? What do your informal advisors say?

Usually by this time in the budget year, the patterns and expectations of the parent organization have been firmly established through the political processes in which its decision makers have been involved. Therefore, you can refine what you have been developing so that it looks reasonable to you and your staff. As you determine which line items must be reduced to conform to probable approvable percentage increases or decreases, you are forced to go back into each activity and service budget and reevaluate.

Are there less costly alternatives that were not in the function budget the first time, which you and your staff might now be willing to consider to reduce the cost of that line item? Are there readjustments between line items that might result in an appropriate shift in the line item totals, making them more satisfactory? Could combinations of program personnel and costs be achieved to reduce total costs? For instance, you have observed a reduction in the work load of your reference librarian, a traditionally invulnerable position in your library. Concurrently, pressures have expanded in your circulation program and you need some peak load assistance there. You might determine that a reduction of the reference librarian to three-quarter time and use of the funds from the other one-fourth salary will help meet the increased circulation demand.

This type of internal reevaluation is a necessary part of the budgeting cycle in order to bring the optimal services into line with the realities of the actual budget.

PREPARING THE FINAL BUDGET

You are now ready for final budget preparation. It seems like a long process, but it's effective, for you know the elements of each program, you understand the issues involved in accomplishing your objectives, and you have the data necessary to build a final budget that is both realistic and salable. In this two-month period, you will sort out the most critically needed activities and services and the most efficient means of providing them. These will be the basis of your final budget, whose development is a result of all the discussions and analyses. You know that even after the formal presentation there may be further changes that your parent organization may demand.

For the moment, you assemble all the parts into a final whole. Figure 4 can be used again, as you work from the activities and services budget figures like those in Chapters 3 and 4 and place the line-item amounts in the required places. At this stage, you again pay particular attention to the percent of increase for each line item. Those above the formally recommended percentages of your parent organization will need special consideration as you develop your budget presentation. Also, the totals (bottom lines) for the whole budget should be reanalyzed . The percentage increase/decrease from each line item of the current year's budget should be computed. Are these percentages within the prescribed or expected limits of increase or decrease, as you understand them? If not, it's back to prioritizing until this is achieved. The alternative approach is to reduce the expenditures in the various functions to meet the decrease/increase percentages. This is not recommended although it is the simplest solution. The results are often unanticipated and unplanned, and may not be those you would choose for your library.

Now you are ready for the next step: development of the budget presentation (as outlined in Chapters 9 and 10). Much of your information is at hand due to the budget planning processes you have already accomplished. Your main objective is to put that material together in an effective presentation package. Consider the people to whom you will present the package. What do *they* think about the library? How may *they* respond to your ideas? How can you relate your ideas to *their* community or school priorities?

Have your staff critique the elements of the presentation. Rewrite, redesign, and improve what you plan to present, and *then* present. You can be confident that you are ready and can respond appropriately with specific answers and information to the questions that will be raised.

Most budgets are submitted to your immediate supervisor and thence on through organizational channels to the chief executive officer (CEO) of your organization. It is well to obtain an organizational chart for the organization to have on hand as an assist in understanding the formal structure with which you interact. Your CEO is usually a city or county manager, a university vice-president or college president, or a school superintendent. Chapter 6 will help you puzzle through many of the issues involved in understanding your organization's formal and informal structures. Budget hearings usually cover the total budgetary needs from the various parts of the organization and integrate them into a total budget for the parent organization. You may expect to be called upon to present your budget at such a hearing. Chapters 9 and 10 are designed to help you with this part of the budget cycle. The budget you have submitted now becomes part of a political process of budgeting. In this process, each subunit of that entity presents a budget and attempts to obtain approval for its organization. In governmental units, police, fire, parks, courts, transportation and so forth are in contention. In universities the various colleges, athletics, student services, maintenance and so forth are the competition. So when you present and request approval for the library budget, you must keep in mind the larger political arena of people and services.

Since your initial planning and development of the budget, other events may have happened in your parent organization. Salary increases may have been negotiated with some subunit and this demands additional funds. Therefore decreases must be taken by other subunits. Some member of a governing board has taken a particular position toward all subunit budgets and you receive a cut in funding because of this. Or, taxpayers have rejected a tax increase that the parent organization had been counting on in the initial budget discussions.

You hope you will receive approval of the budget as presented. Often, however, changes must be made as a result of the presentation and review. If these changes would necessitate a major overhaul of a portion of the budget, use the information you have developed to describe to the decision makers the impact such changes will make on the ability of the library to fulfill its purposes. Then make sure all parties agree on the budget and what it will provide for the subsequent year. You may expect a formal communication from the parent organization shortly with a copy of your approved budget.

You are now ready to implement the budget with the beginning of the fiscal year and to manage it effectively. Chapters 11 and 12 deal with this process.

PRACTICE EXPERIENCES

1. Reproduce figure 1 from memory.
2. Discuss why it takes almost a full year to develop an effective library budget.
3. List at least four reasons why "chance remarks" are important in integrating planning information into your budget.
4. List the issues that will be important to you in prioritizing your library programs.
5. Discuss the importance of the "cut line" in budgeting.

6. List at least five ways in which an understanding of the budget cycle can help you to be a more effective library manager when you face budget recisions.

SELECTED REFERENCES

Childers, Thomas A., and Nancy A. Van House. *What's Good? Describing Your Public Library's Effectiveness.* Chicago: American Library Association, 1993.

Heymann, Philip B. *Politics of Public Management.* New Haven, Conn.: Yale University Press, 1987.

McClure, Charles, Amy Owen, Douglas L. Zweizig, Mary Jo Lynch, and Nancy A. Van House. *Planning and Role Setting for Public Libraries.* Chicago: American Library Association, 1987.

McClure, Charles, et al. *Planning for Library Services.* New York: Hawthorne Press, 1982.

Mitzberg, Henry. *Mitzberg on Management: Inside Our Strange World of Organizations.* New York: Free Press, 1989.

2
Needs Assessment and Planning

WHY DOES YOUR LIBRARY EXIST?

All libraries are committed to meeting the community's information needs, and all public libraries share a common mission of meeting the community's cultural, educational, and recreational needs as well.

But the needs of each community differ so that the roles of each library will emphasize different activities and services to different clientele.

Your ability to define and describe your library to its funding agency and to its various stakeholders is one of the important functions you must discharge. This is increasingly significant when funding is extremely competitive due to decreases in available dollars. Following the processes suggested herein, the budget you prepare will be based on objectives that you plan to accomplish. The beginning point for these objectives is the description of the roles that your library will play in the community.

The processes developed by McClure, et al., in *Planning and Role Setting for Public Libraries* will assist you in developing the roles and mission of your library. Choosing from among the eight roles McClure lists is the beginning step. (McClure, *Planning and Role Setting*, p. 28.) The entire planning process summarized in this work is an excellent foundation for the development of your budget. The roles, once identified and agreed upon in your library planning, provide the basis for the development of your mission statement. The process that then begins provides the linkage between the needs and the activities of the library. The planning system extends to developing objectives for the library, with their attendant evaluative criteria. The budgeting system then moves from these objectives to create a structure that identifies the funds

15

necessary for the fiscal support of these objectives. The stucture below demonstrates the necessary marriage between the two vital systems—planning and budgeting.

PLANNING	BUDGETING
Mission	Functions
Roles	Programs
Goals	
Objectives ←→	Activities
	Services

The objectives to be achieved by the library are accomplished through specific activities and services, for which costs are identified. Activities are the *essential* elements of the library operation. Services are the added nonessential offerings of the library. Various activities and services are categorized into groups of "programs" and these programs into the broader "functions" of the library. Chapter 4 deals in-depth with this structural conceptualization.

To help identify your library's roles, you will need to gather some basic data:

A community profile (community characteristics)
A listing of the library's current activities and services
    (library characteristics)
Measures of the performance of the library (objectives)

Workform C (McClure, pp. 90–93) and Chapter 5 of that work will be of particular help in dealing with these issues. Alternatively, using Dimension 1 as found in *What's Good?* (Childers and Van House, p. 61), assists with similar developments, but in a different way. The McClure approach is more consistent with the approach of this text. However, the key issue is gathering appropriate data to provide the foundation for the budgeting process, i.e., a description of the library in analytical terms.

COMMUNITY PROFILE

A community profile summarizes the population, industries, and services available in a community. This information can be found in secondary sources, especially census data, but also in reports prepared by the Chamber of Commerce, local planning documents, and the advertising departments of local newspapers, etc.

Imagine the case of a branch librarian, noted for her excellent children's program, who noticed a sharp decline in program attendance. The director was sure the librarian had "lost her touch." She, on the other hand, blamed the intolerance of some of her elderly patrons for frightening the children away. After examining trends in the ages of neighborhood residents and household sizes through census data, they both realized that the predominance of households had changed to single-member households and the elderly population had increased considerably. Young families were moving into the north side of the city where low-cost housing was going up. Once the library director understood the facts, it was easy to make staffing and operational decisions for both the South and North branches of the library.

Census Data

The census data most useful to library managers are census tracts. Having a population averaging 4,000, census tracts are fairly homogeneous with respect to population characteristics, economic status, and living conditions. Census tract data are now available on CD ROM. Your state library can provide you with maps of the census tracts in your service area. Using the data for the tracts served by your library, you can easily determine race, gender, educational and income levels, occupations, and household sizes for each area you serve. Figure 5 provides a way to organize the census information that will be most useful to you.

Other Information

Population characteristics are not the only data to consider. Information on business and industry can also be crucial. For example, a director of a library was puzzled by the heavy circulation of romances when census data showed a concentration of highly educated professionals in the area served. After securing business/industry information, she realized that hundreds of the expected library users were commuting to work outside the community. The library was serving the information needs of the remaining, less highly educated population. Now the director realized why romances were popular, and changed library emphases to meet the information needs of this public.

Along with population characteristics and data about business and industry, the community profile should reveal the existence of social clubs, recreational facilities, cultural activities, and community and special interest groups. If your city lacks organized activities, you may want to pursue special services and promote use of the library's meeting rooms. But if there are numerous clubs and groups, your efforts to

Figure 5. Organizing Census Information

	Census Tract			Community	
	1970	1980	1990	1990	Census Tract as Percent of Community
Total Population	___	___	___	___	___
Percent of population change each decade	___	___	___	___	___
Percent of population over 25	___	___	___	___	___
Median age of population	___	___	___	___	___
Percent of population over 25 with less than 12 years school completed	___	___	___	___	___
With high school graduation	___	___	___	___	___
13+ years school completed	___	___	___	___	___
Median years school completed	___	___	___	___	___
Median family income	___	___	___	___	___

provide services that may duplicate what is already available may be unnecessary. Take note of educational facilities, museums, and other types of libraries. By developing your relationship with those other information resources, you may gain insights into possibilities of resource sharing and nonduplication of efforts.

LIBRARY OPERATIONS

A community profile will give you general background to help determine the library's potential roles in the community. Some data will not be useful to you as a decision maker until they can be paired with information on current library operations.

You are probably already collecting statistics on current library operations as a part of the Federal-State Cooperative Data Services and perhaps Public Library Data Service. To assist you with interpretation, these data should be prepared annually and then cumulated to reveal year-to-year trends over a five-year period. Data collected can then be summarized in a format like that suggested in figure 6. Additional categories are added to include all of the output measures found on Workform C, Part D. (McClure, p. 93.)

A few examples may illustrate this information.

What does it mean to have 2,000 people registered? Nothing at all, until you calculate your registrants as a percentage of the community's population. Two thousand registered borrowers are 80 percent of a population of 2,500, but only 2 percent of 100,000. However, 2 percent of the population may be significant if that represents an increase from the year before. The increase is calculated by dividing the number of registrants during the current year by the number of registrants last year (in this example, 1,500), then subtracting 1.

$$2,000 \; / \; 1,500 = 1.33$$
$$1.33 \; - \; 1 = \; .33$$

This is a 33 percent increase in registrations.

On the maps of census tracts, pinpoint the location of each of the library's facilities. What can you learn from studying the physical area surrounding them? Large highways, railroad facilities, rivers and so forth are often barriers for potential patrons. This is particularly true for children. Additionally, ideas suggested in Dimension 5 (Childers, pp. 48–49) are of significance in looking at library facilities.

Sources of Income

Why do you care about the sources of income as long as you are getting the money? A chart like figure 6 will help you compare the percentage of funds from different sources over a five-year period. Each year, calculate the part of the total coming from local, state, and federal sources, gifts, and miscellaneous revenues. You will be able to note any significant increases or decreases in support from source to source. The finance committee may then be informed that federal or state revenues are steadily decreasing, so that they are challenged to appropriate enough money locally to maintain levels of service. As budget reductions increasingly make an impact on your library operations your data becomes the foundation for your decision making about when and where to shift emphasis.

Figure 6. Five-Year Analysis of Data

	1989	1990	1991	1992	1993
Income, by source					
Local	___	___	___	___	___
State	___	___	___	___	___
Federal	___	___	___	___	___
Gifts	___	___	___	___	___
Other	___	___	___	___	___
Total	___	___	___	___	___
Total income per capita	___	___	___	___	___
Expenditure, by category					
Personnel services	___	___	___	___	___
Benefits	___	___	___	___	___
Materials and Supplies	___	___	___	___	___
Capital outlay	___	___	___	___	___
Total	___	___	___	___	___
Registered borrowers					
Adult	___	___	___	___	___
Juvenile	___	___	___	___	___
Total	___	___	___	___	___
Percent of total population	___	___	___	___	___
Circulation of materials					
Adult	___	___	___	___	___
Juvenile	___	___	___	___	___
Total	___	___	___	___	___
Total circ. per capita	___	___	___	___	___
Total circ. per registered borrower	___	___	___	___	___
Total circ. per volume	___	___	___	___	___
OR					
Circulation of materials					
Print materials	___	___	___	___	___
Nonprint materials	___	___	___	___	___
Total	___	___	___	___	___
Volumes, beginning of year					
Total	___	___	___	___	___
Added	___	___	___	___	___
Weeded	___	___	___	___	___
Volumes, end of year					
Total	___	___	___	___	___
Adult	___	___	___	___	___
Juvenile	___	___	___	___	___
Total	___	___	___	___	___
Titles, end of year					
Adult	___	___	___	___	___
Juvenile	___	___	___	___	___
Total	___	___	___	___	___
Titles per capita	___	___	___	___	___

Per Capita Income

Your total budget becomes more meaningful when you compute it on a per capita basis and calculate its purchasing power. These figures can be charted to show increases and decreases over a five-year period.

Per capita income is computed by dividing the library's total income by the total population:

$$\$380,000 \ / \ 50,000 = \$7.60$$

If last year's per capita income had been $7.80, the decrease was 3 percent:

$$\$7.60 \ / \ \$7.80 = .0974$$
$$.0974 - 1 = .026, \text{ roughly } 3\%$$

Any decrease in per capita support means little until you discover how much that reduced purchasing power provides compared to last year's budget, taking inflation into account. Determine the inflation rate by referencing the Consumer Price Index (CPI). For 1990 and 1991 the CPI rose about 5 percent per year.

Inflation was 5 percent, so every dollar of 1992 income was worth only 95 cents of every 1991 dollar. By multiplying the 1992 per capita income by 95 percent, you can calculate the increase or decrease in real dollars from 1991 to 1992:

$$\$7.60 \times .95 = \$7.22$$
$$\$7.22 \ / \ \$7.40 = .976$$

Thus the income appropriated in 1992/93 is worth 97.6 percent of that appropriated during 1991. In this hypothetical situation, there has been a 2.4 percent decrease in real purchasing power. You now have to think about a 5.4 percent reduction in the budget. (Figure 7 and exercise 4 will help you understand these calculations.)

Expenditures

For each of your budgeted items (personnel services, materials and supplies, capital outlay, etc.) identify the percentage of total expenditures annually and over a five-year period as in figure 6. Compare these trends with the dollar trends in figure 7, and also with your knowledge of the library's priorities. Do your rising personnel and utility costs reflect these priorities? Are there other substantial changes? Do the trends you observe reflect the direction in which your library is intended to move? Note discrepancies between the trends you observe and the goals and objectives that you, your staff, and your board are pursuing.

These are the challenges you must meet as you plan and replan your budget.

Figure 7. Calculating Real-Income Changes

Year	Total Income	Per Capita Income	Percent of Change	CPI at Midyear	Percent of Real-Dollar Increase or Decrease
1988	____	____	____	____	____
1989	____	____	____	____	____
1990	____	____	____	____	____
1991	____	____	____	____	____
1992	____	____	____	____	____
1993	____	____	____	____	____

NOW WHAT?

You now have a community profile and a five-year analysis of library statistics. Pulling the supporting data together is time consuming. Once done, however, the community profile may not have to be revised until new census data are available. The five-year analysis of library statistics needs only to be kept up to date. Use this information as support data to identify your library's roles in the community.

You will need to measure library performance. The development of performance measures as recommended by McClure, et. al., in Chapter 5 of *Planning and Role Setting*, enhances your ability to relate expenditures to the outcomes that are developed through this process.

Remember, the roles chosen by different libraries will vary. Therefore, the goals statements of different libraries will vary.

Begin by reviewing any existing library goals statement. Too often, goal statements have been developed as a response to organizational pressures without reference to objective data. They sound good, but they may not be effective for library planning. Ask yourself these questions as you review the goal statements.

Do they provide the scope necessary to respond to the library's chosen roles?

Are they broad enough to provide direction for planning?

Are they supported by the data collected in the community profile
and the library's statistics?

Do they need to be changed to accomplish any or all of the three
questions above?

As discussions about the goals of your library progress, remember that
the goal statements should include who is to be served and through what
types of service. These statements may support the status quo or may
define changes in direction.

For example, a school library that recognizes that there is an accessible public library, well stocked to meet the recreational reading needs
of its students, may decide:

"The library will make available materials supportive of the curriculum to its students and teachers."

Another school library, emphasizing library-use instruction and reference activities, may decide:

"The library will provide information, curriculum-related materials, and instruction in the use of the library to the students and
teachers of the school."

After the goals have been identified, the development of objectives is
undertaken. The approach suggested in *Planning and Role Setting* will be
very helpful at this point. While objective development is a demanding
activity, after the first year you will have to deal only with changes that
occur. Remember also that the objectives become the interface between
the planning and the budgeting systems and therefore are vital to both
structures. They provide the basis for evaluating the effectiveness of your
library, describing it to the various stakeholders, and developing and
defending your budget.

SUMMARY

It is easy to say that libraries exist to provide informational, recreational,
educational, and cultural opportunities to their communities. But it is
more demanding to say why a particular library exists in a specific
community: why it is important and why it should be funded at some
particular level.

To provide these answers, you need to gather information about your
community, about current library operations and performance.

Each library will identify different roles for itself, ones that are tied in with the makeup of its community. From these general direction-giving roles, specific objectives will be developed. As discussed, roles and objectives have a vital relationship to the budgeting process.

PRACTICE EXPERIENCES

1. Locate maps and data on census tracts served by your library or school. If you are not a working librarian, do so for the neighborhood in which you live.

2. Complete the first three columns of figure 6 for the census tract in which your library, school, or home is located.

3. Complete the fourth and fifth columns of figure 6, comparing the 1990 census tract data with the 1990 population characteristics of the community as a whole.

4. Calculate the per capita income for your library (or one on which you can get information) for each year from 1988 to 1993. Calculate the percentage increase or decrease in per capita support over the five-year period.

5. Obtain or create a mission statement for a library. Critique this statement. Does it develop a rational direction for the library? Rewrite the statement so that it provides a usable base for library development.

SELECTED READINGS

Childers, Thomas A., and Nancy A. Van House. *What's Good? Describing Your Public Library's Effectiveness.* Chicago: American Library Association, 1993.

DeProspo, Earnest R., Ellen Altman, and Kenneth E. Beasley. *Performance Measures for Public Libraries.* Chicago: Public Library Association, American Library Association, 1973.

Jackson, Inez L., and E. Ramsey. *Library Planning and Budgeting.* New York: Franklin Watts, 1986.

McClure, Charles, Amy Owen, Douglas L. Zweizig, Mary Jo Lynch, Nancy A. Van House. *Planning and Role Setting for Public Libraries.* Chicago: American Library Association, 1987.

Plamour, Vernon E., Marcia C. Bellassai, and Nancy V. DeWath. *A Planning Process for Public Libraries.* Chicago: American Library Association, 1980.

Public Library Association Goals, Guidelines, and Standards Committee, *The Public Library Mission Statement and Its Imperatives for Service.* Chicago: American Library Association, 1979.

Tomor, Christinger. "The Effects of Recession in Academic and Public Libraries," *The Bowker Annual: Library and Book Trade Almanac*. New Providence, NJ:
R. R. Bowker, 1992.

U.S. Department of Commerce, Bureau of the Census, *County Business Patterns*.

U.S. Department of Commerce, Bureau of the Census, *General Population Characteristics, 1990 Census of Population*.

Van House, Nancy A., Mary Jo Lynch, Charles R. McClure, Douglas L. Zweizig,
and Eleanor Jo Roger. *Output Measures for Public Libraries*, 2nd ed. Chicago:
American Library Association, 1992.

3
Line-Item Budgeting

OVERVIEW OF LINE-ITEM BUDGETING

The line-item budget (sometimes called expenditure budget) is the most commonly used format for budgeting, probably because of its long history and the ease with which one year's expenses can be compared with the next. Line items are typically separated into categories such as personnel, equipment, supplies, materials and so forth.

There has been a long tradition of incrementalism in both budgeting and decision making—small changes, made a bit at a time, over time. An expanding economy with an expanding tax base fostered this incrementalism: anticipating the rate of expansion and adding that factor to the budget each year. This tradition is reflected by line-item budgets, each line of which is increased or decreased a little bit each year, with no questions asked about the increase or decrease in services those expenditures are expected to provide. Recision budgeting usually takes the form of percentage decreases in line-item categories. For instance, from a CEO point of view and from the politics of that position it is usually easier to reduce the personnel line by 5 percent than to spend the massive amount of time and energy it would take to recover the same amount of funds in other ways.

The line-item budget format usually summarizes a four-year period: expenditures of the prior years (usually 2 years), with estimates for the current year and the request for the next year. Figure 8 is a basic line-item budget sheet. You will notice that the current year has three columns, "appropriation budget," "amended budget" and "estimated expenditures." This is true for any year that is in operation. The appropriation column contains the figures approved before the beginning of the fiscal year. The amended budget is the approved budget as changed during the fiscal year. The estimated expenditures are the funds actually used during that year. The expended budget cannot be completed until the year is over and the fiscal records of that year are finally tabulated. Therefore, the expenditures are "estimated" during the later part of the fiscal year as you are developing the subsequent year's budget proposal. This four-year summary makes it easy to compare amounts of money from one year to the next. Large differences are usually questioned by the finance committee and small, incremental increases or decreases are generally unchallenged.

However, when organizations face decreasing funds, incrementalism becomes a questionable practice. Be very careful to be attuned to the attitude of your parent organization regarding incrementalism as a part of your budget preparation. (See Chapter 6 for further information about how to access organizational attitudes and expectations.)

Line-item budgets are normally divided into a few universally used general accounts that are subdivided according to the specific needs of the organization. The line-item format's usefulness as a summary is one reason it is used to summarize the costs of each program in a budget.

The budget is separated into two areas: operating expenses and capital outlay. Capital outlay, as discussed in this text, relates to outlays for equipment for the library. Capital outlay for major remodeling or for the constructing and equipping of new buildings is often handled over several fiscal years and involves many complexities. We will not deal with this long-term capital outlay budgeting. Incurred in the course of ordinary activities of the library, operating expenses include personnel services, materials and supplies, contractual services, office expenses and so forth. These items receive annual appropriations, that are expended annually. In a cash budgeting system, neither expenses nor appropriations can be carried over from one year to the next. Capital outlay for other than equipment is often budgeted over years and both expenses and appropriations may be carried forward. For instance, the planning and constructing of a new library usually takes several years and money must be committed at the beginning of the cycle for its construction and equipment.

All systems of accounting require a description of the way money is expended. Organizations large enough to support a library have standardized these into line items. So you will encounter line items almost universally.

Your parent organization will have a description of each of the line items used in its budgeting system with the definitions that apply. Make sure to obtain these descriptions and use them in your budget preparation, presentation, and management at all times.

Following are the fund accounts most commonly used in line-item budgets.

Figure 8. Basic Line-Item Budget Sheet

Account Number	Account Title	Actual Expenditures, FY '91	Actual Expenditures, FY '92	Appropriation, FY '93	Amended Budget Dec. '93	Estimated Expenditures, FY '93	Requested for FY '94
100	Personnel services						
200	Employee benefits						
300	Materials & supplies						
400	Contractual services						
500	Purchased/lease equipment						
600	Capital outlay						
	Total						

FUND ACCOUNTS

Personnel Services

Salaries may be considered one by one or grouped by type of employee: librarian, technical, clerical, and custodial. You identify each person, each job title, budgeted salary for the prior period, salary actually paid to date (usually through the first quarter or two of the current fiscal year), and next year's requested salary.

It is not unusual for personnel costs in labor-intensive operations to be greater than 50 percent of the budget (Eckard, p. 332). In some service organizations salaries may account for 70 to 75 percent of the total budget. In the library the impact of increasing automation probably will impact this figure over the next decade. A survey of public libraries for fiscal year 1978 revealed that "staff accounted for the largest expenditure for all public libraries." (Eckard, p. 329.) Salary increases are not discretionary. They are usually derived from a wage scale prepared by the parent organization, negotiated with a union, or determined by the parent organization as a specific percentage increase. The numbers of employees and their job descriptions are more subject to negotiation and manipulation.

Employee Benefits

Employers pay part or all of their worker's benefits such as insurance, retirement, and social security. If benefits are paid from the general fund, you may not have to budget for them; otherwise you have to account for them in your budget. There may be one line for benefits, or the account may be divided by benefit type: insurance, retirement, FICA. Retirement and FICA are usually percentages, applied to the employee's salary; insurance costs vary with the individual's coverage. Your parent organization will provide you with the basis for deriving these figures if you are to include them in your budget information.

Materials and Supplies

Here you budget for all custodial, electrical, plumbing, and office supplies, as well as book, serial, and audiovisual purchases. This will probably be the second largest amount of money budgeted, and may represent about 15 percent of a public library's appropriation (Eckard, pp. 334–335).

Contractual Services

Rent and maintenance contracts on buildings and equipment, and service contracts on such things as cataloging, binding, or consulting are contractual or purchased services. This category is sometimes called *purchased services.*

Purchased/Lease Equipment

Not to be confused with contractual services, this line item includes only equipment leased for purchase at a later date. Some parent organizations are prohibited by law to enter into purchased/lease agreements for equipment. Make sure of your parent organization's position in regard to this category.

Capital Outlay

This outlay represents expenditures for the acquisition of long-term assets such as audiovisual apparatus, remodeling or improvements, equipment, furniture for new construction, and automotive vehicles.

Categorical Funds

Included in this fund are monies with designated uses, such as federal and state grants. Such funds usually will have their own line-item budgets and will often operate as if they were a library activity or service. However, since they are approved by the granting agency, the approval for the amounts included in the various line items lies with that agency and not with your parent organization. Therefore these funds are usually shown in your budget as the single line item "categorical funds."

REFINING BUDGET ACCOUNTS

You are not stuck with budget accounts just because they have been used in the past. Your common sense will reveal categories unique to your organization. For example, only a library hires pages. Account 150, which deals with pages, was developed specifically for use by a library.

Think about the regular reports you will have to prepare for the state library, the school district, or other funding agencies. By planning ahead, you may be able to design your budget format to routinely gather data to easily complete these reports. Definitions of what may and may not be charged to each line item differ from one organization to another. You may find it difficult to decide whether a purchase is considered equipment or supply. In general, supplies are consumable; they may have to be replaced or replenished within a specified time. Equipment is long lasting. Some parent organizations base the difference on cost alone: anything under a specified amount may be a supply; over that amount, equipment. You must know your organization's definitions and how to apply them as you create and expend your budget.

Organizations differ in their definitions of what is to be included in each line item. Discuss the use and definition of accounts with the chief accountant of your parent organization or with your state library consultant. Do this before the beginning of a budget year so you can be ready to account for expenditures as they occur.

FOCUS ON RESOURCES, NOT RESULTS

Line-item budgets focus on resources. While an expense is assigned to each account, there is no identifiable relationship between money and achievements. For instance, there is no way to tell whether the amount to be spent for personnel equals the results achieved through their efforts. Neither is the focus of their activities identified in this type of budget. Managers, however, do adapt their line items to improve results in their operations. For instance, shifting salary resources for technical personnel in the library and thereby saving funds that might have been spent for more expensive professional personnel may free funds to use for additional library services.

Line-item budgets are somewhat flexible. For example, the general account called Personnel Services may be assigned the account number 100. The specific types of employees may be divided as follows: librarians, account 110; technical, 120; clerical, 130; and custodial, 140. You usually have some flexibility among the 100-level accounts. If you overspend in 120 and underspend in 130, it will probably be unchallenged as long as the money allocated for the entire Personnel Services account is neither over- nor underspent. But you would have to return to your funding board to get permission to pay unexpectedly high utility bills (account 415) from the unexpended account 100 funds.

There are two premises on which line-item budgeting proceeds: base and fair share. "The base is the general expectation among the participants that programs will be carried on at close to the going level of expenditures." (Wildavsky, p. 17.) It is generally accepted that once a program or item is budgeted, you can expect that it is accepted and will not be questioned again. It is not often that a budget line item is totally eliminated. However, in periods of recision many line items are slowly eroded until they may contain relatively few funds. If your parent organization encounters a shortfall in revenues during the operational year, you may be instructed to review all of your line items for possible recision of your approved budget amounts.

Fair share refers to the expectation that the library's budget will get roughly the same proportion of funds (above or below its established base) as is received by all other city or school departments. Each line item is expected, in turn, to receive its fair-share proportion of increase or decrease in funds also. If a 3 percent recision is announced by your parent organization, it is generally felt that 3 percent should be applied to each line item to be "fair." Sometimes organizations require this. You must be vigilant in this regard and argue for where the least harm will be done. A 3 percent recision in contract services might not be possible due to contracts already signed and funds thereby committed. However, changes in personnel may have resulted in adequate fund availability to cover the entire 3 percent recision.

Line-item budgets lend themselves to incremental increase, and you can use the concept of incrementalism to your advantage in a number of ways. For example, funding board members find it easy to analyze line-item budgets by noticing increases or decreases in accounts from year to year. You can benefit from their analysis by identifying growth or establishing need, whichever is more persuasive.

Items that lack public support or understanding may be approved for funding by being placed in large categories so they can't be singled out. For example, your use data may show increasing interest in tape cassettes and CD ROMs and a corresponding decline in use of print materials by students; but you know your voting population will disapprove of your emphasis on nonprint sources. Therefore, you may wish to lump all audiovisual purchases with print materials into a general line item "Library Materials."

The line-item budget, so widely used, is the foundation for other types of budgets. In Chapters 4 and 5 you will find how both Function Budgets and Zero Base Budgets are organized in their internal structure based on line-item concepts. Therefore, acquaint yourself thoroughly with the line-item budget's advantages and disadvantages. By using it well, you will enhance your image and effectiveness as a fiscal manager.

Later chapters on expenditure and revenue projection detail the development of a line-item budget.

PRACTICE EXPERIENCES

1. Develop a detailed list of the categories on your line-item budget during the last three years. Include special accounts and changes made from year to year. Revise the list by developing what you consider the most effective set of ideal categories. Compare this list with your current year's budget.

2. Explain why line-item budgeting is so commonly used.

3. Using your answer to 1 above, identify line items that are specific to the library. Describe why you think this is so.

SELECTED READINGS

Eckard, Helen M. "NCES Survey of Public Libraries, 1977–78." *Bowker Annual,* 27th ed. New York: Bowker, 1982.

Robbins, Jane B., and Douglas L. Zweizig. *Keeping the Books: Public Library Financial Practices.* Fort Atkinson, Wis.: Highsmith Press, 1992.

Sweeny, H.W., and Robert Rachlin, *Handbook of Budgeting: Systems and Controls for Financial Management.* New York: Ronald, 1981.

Wildavsky, Aaron. *Budgeting: A Comparative Theory of Budgetary Processes.* Boston: Little, 1975.

———. *The Politics of the Budgetary Process,* 3rd ed. Boston: Little, 1979.

4
Budgeting by Functions

THE CONCEPT OF BUDGETING

The concept of budgeting in terms of the way an organization functions, that is, by assigning funds to the "programs" of the organization, was developed during the 1960s and 1970s. Initially it was called Programming, Planning and Budgeting Systems (PPBS). Somewhat later it became PPBES, adding Evaluation to the list. The concept was to tie the budget to the planning process, and through the assignment of funds, to track the functions of the organization. Thus, from planning through evaluation of each function there would be accountability related to costs. Program budgeting was well described and applications were proposed for many types of organizations, including the library. (Lee, 1973.)

As is often the case with management trends, PPBES fell out of vogue. The economy was in a growth mode, and it was simpler to continue to follow the path of least resistance—incrementalism within the line-item budget.

Times have changed, and different approaches are called for. The trend to emphasize planning as a significant part of managing the library has grown in favor. "Those who control the planning and budgeting processes in organizations and use them to effective ends are likely to succeed in the future and those who cannot will, in all probability, fail." (McClure, et al., 1982, p. 183.)

This chapter emphasizes the use of "function" budgeting, a term more descriptive of the way libraries work. The term "program" in the library means something different from the term "program" in program budgeting. To minimize confusion, the term "function" will be used here as the basis for budget organization. This chapter will develop a budget structure that can be used to utilize the planning output presented in Chapter 2.

Key Definitions

Unless there is an effective set of definitions for all of the functions, programs, activities and services of the library, there is no effective way to begin to prioritize. Without prioritization there is no effective way to undertake recision budgeting or to compare the costs and significance of library activities and services. Without a methodology, it is possible that essential functions of the library will be diluted and less essential functions will be maintained. The following definitions have not been articulated in the literature, but they are necessary for the understanding and use of the contents of this text.

Functions: The groupings of essential activities of the library.

Programs: The first subdivision of functions, further categorizing the essential activities of the library.

Activities: The library exists for these and without them the very nature of the library would be changed. The scope of an activity or its intensity can be changed as long as the activity remains within a program.

Services: Added offerings of the library to meet specific challenges or needs of the library. These are not essential to the nature of the library. They may be a subset of either Activities or Programs.

FUNCTION BUDGETING

Often in a world short on budget funds, you will be called upon to make budget cutbacks due to shortfalls in funding or lack of funding availability. You may need to go back during the budgetary year and make further cuts in your activities and services. It is not unusual to be told by your funding agency that you must plan on reduced funds for the ensuing budget year. Additionally, there may be portions of the library operation which, based on your planning efforts, need to be modified or deleted. Any of these situations will cause a major change in your library operation. You must make clear decisions about where to cut and why, or how to restructure. A function based budget format will assist you in making the best of such difficult situations. This chapter and Chapter 5 provide a rational basis for such decisions.

If you receive a mandate to cut back during a given year (do a recision budget), one of your critical decisions will be where to cut so that you will cause the least damage to the library. Therefore, you should think in a long-term mode rather than just the rest of the current year. You must assess the impact on your overall planning structure and the operations of the library.

A significant question when you begin the budgeting process is where to start. What will be the basis for organizing your efforts? How will you begin? What steps must be taken to develop a defensible, realistic budget to present to your funding agency? When funding money is in short supply and the library must compete with others for its survival how can its highest priorities be identified and supported appropriately?

Often librarians and other managers begin by looking back at the budgets of preceding years to determine what has been done. This is a positive way to begin, for it provides a sense of the budgetary history of the organization.

However, once some very basic observations have been made about those previous years' budgets, the first question comes back again: What will be the basis of my budgeting efforts? Most budgets that you will encounter are in what is commonly described as *line-item format*, where expenditures are categorized according to kinds of things and services purchased, regardless of how they are used by the library.

What is needed in the budget is some method of identifying what is going on, what is being accomplished, how the use of money achieves outcomes, and how the role of the library is carried out in the community. Additionally, a way to differentiate the critical significance of various library "programs" is called for. The definitions of function, programs, activities and services provided in the early part of this chapter form the foundation of all such budgeting activities. The process described in this chapter will assist you in dealing with many of these fundamental budgeting questions. At the end of the chapter you will also find an example of the way the function budgeting process may be put to work to deal with such issues. With these ideas in mind, let's explore the elements of *function budgeting*.

Elements of Function Budgeting

Function budgets relate the expenditures of the library to the services they provide, like the common library functions of administration, public service or technical service, etc. However, functions may alternatively be defined by clientele served or by service units. In general, the aim of the function budget is to show how much the library spends on each of its activities and services.

In contrast, the line-item budget shows what the library spends on the goods and services it acquires.

The line-item format is incorporated into the program budget format, as indicated in figure 9. By identifying expenditure categories for each activity or service, you end with miniline-item budgets that can then be compiled and transferred into either a comprehensive line-item format or a function budget. Even if your final budget must be in line-item format, it is easier for you the manager/librarian to make changes if it is built from the function budget approach.

Function budgets look like minibudgets that support each of the library's identified activities and services. Each has line-item amounts focused on the resources needed to achieve the goals of every activity or service of the library.

Figure 9 indicates how these concepts of line items and functions are related in the function budget format. As you see, each function will include many line items. Every line item is not always needed for every function. The lines on the chart represent a few that usually are found in a completed line-item budget. The functions also are representative of those that may ultimately be included in a complete function budget.

Figure 9. Basic Function Budget

Function	I									II
Program		A			B					
Activity			1				1			Etc.
Services				a				a		
Services					2				2	
Line items:										
Personnel										
Employee benefits										
Materials										
Periodicals										
Supplies										
Books										
Etc.										
TOTALS										

Detailed descriptions of line-item budgeting and expenditure projection are found in Chapters 3 and 7.

Function budgeting is stressed in this text because it offers a number of managerial advantages:

It coordinates with the library's planning process.

It identifies money spent on the activities and services stressed by the library's role statements.

It assists in prioritizing dollar commitments to your functions when funding is cut and budget recisions are required.

It helps you decide how best to meet needs when there is a gap between current and desired activity and service levels.

It offers you a management tool helpful in making activity and service related changes.

Steps in Function Budgeting Process

The function budgeting process is carried out in six basic steps:

Identify the functions and their goals. The goals should be clearly related to the library's roles that were identified during the planning process.

Project changes in each program for the coming year by setting objectives to meet the desired outcomes of each activity or service within the program, evaluating alternative ways of meeting the objectives, and selecting the ways to meet them.

Prepare a line-item budget for each activity and service.

Rank the activities and services by order of importance, according to their relevance to the library's roles in the community.

Compile the budgets of the functions into the final function budget for the entire library.

Evaluate both the budgeting process and whether the funded activities and services accomplished their established objectives. This step relates the budget back to the planning system.

IDENTIFYING ACTIVITIES AND SERVICES

Activities or services are defined as a focus of organizational effort that can be defined separately and for which specific sets of objectives can be developed. The activities and services identified are somewhat different in every organization or from public to academic libraries. The pattern used in this chapter is merely illustrative, and should not be used without modification. Your library setting may be different enough to justify a unique approach. For instance, the very differences in the structure of an organization will have some impact on the way activity and service categories might be identified. A public library would develop activity and service categories that are different from a school library. The issue is to study carefully the library for which the budget is being developed, and list each possible activity and service category.

Establishing the basis on which activities and services are defined is critical to the entire process. Programs are usually defined by the functions the library staff perform: administration, technical services, and public services. In every case, there should be a direct link between the library's roles statements and its functions.

Next, identify the programs that operate under each function. For instance, under technical services there may be located acquisitions, cataloging, and database management.

Now, identify the activities that fall under each program. As in Figure 10, under cataloging we find original cataloging, and under database management we find discarding records and authority files. Finally, within each activity identify the services that are being offered. For instance, under periodical selection (reference), a special service for selection of periodicals related to Hispanic Americans might be identified. Occasionally there are services that relate to a program category directly rather than being a subsystem of an activity.

If categories are not clearly defined, expected results cannot be clearly described. Lack of clarity in function, program, activity and services identification may cause confusion and misdirection of resources. Ultimately, the final evaluations will not identify real achievements. Accurate identification leads to clear objectives and evaluations. It allows you to communicate results more easily understood by your parent agency and the various library stakeholders.

Identifying Categories

To identify categories, list all of those that come to mind for your library. Ask your staff to do the same independently. Collect all the lists and post the items on a large wallboard so that everyone can add whatever he or she thinks necessary.

EXAMPLE A. CATEGORIES OF THE LIBRARY

> Buy books
> Circulate materials
> Teach people to use the card catalog
> Answer reference questions
> Cataloging and classification

Figure 10. Library Functions, Programs, Activities, and Services (example)

Function	Program	Activity	Services
Public Services	Circulation	Reserves	Faculty requests Text books Multiple copies Articles, Books
		Overdues, Interlibrary loan, Library cards Photocopy services	

	Reference	Reader services	Books
			    Reference tool
			    Curriculum
			Support
			    Recreational

		Library instruction Information services	CD-ROMs

		Collection development
		    Monograph/book
		Selection
		    Periodical selection
		    Weeding, Planning
			On-line searching

Technical Services	Acquisitions	Materials ordering Materials receiving Continuations/serials Copy editing	

	Cataloging	Original cataloging	Print materials
			    Books
			    Periodicals
			Nonprint materials
			    Video, Software

	Database Management	Discarding records Authority files, Union catalog, Preparation Library liaison	
Administration	Budget	Unit budget oversite Branch budget oversite	

	Personnel	Selection
		Training
			Travel to
			    conferences
			    workshops

	Facilities Planning	Evaluation
		Site selection, Final
		    planning, Construction
		Furniture selection
			Continuing
			    education

EXAMPLE A. CATEGORIES OF THE LIBRARY (continued)
> Ordering materials
> Cleaning the building
> Story hours
> Exhibits
> Crafts programs
> Place to study
> An escape from home
> Attend meetings and watch movies
> Shelving and redoing shelves
> Weeding
> Getting back issues of magazines people request
> Overdues
> Interlibrary loans
> Access to on-line databases
> Adult programs
> Bookmobile service
> Video cassettes to circulate

Compare the results of your planning documents (Chapter 2) with the listings on the wallchart. Continue to combine, compile, and refine these categories until you think you have considered them all. Try to follow the pattern:

> Function
> > Program
> > > Activity
> > > > Service (subset under Activity)
> > > > Service (occasionally—subset under Program)

Attempt to classify all of the items that have been listed. It is not an easy task, nor one in which you will find total agreement. The most heated discussions will probably center around the essentiality question. If something is essential to the library it is an *activity,* if it is not essential it is a *service.* This distinction, as you will observe, is what drives the organization of the budget. Therefore, continue to pursue the exercise until you have clearly made these distinctions. Remember, this is the foundation of your budget. Your flexible items will be your activities and services. Your fixed items are your functions and programs.

Assume a part of the mission statement reads:

> "The library will continue to provide educational, informational, and recreational activities to all children and adults of the city, and will develop outreach services for the aging, handicapped, and functionally illiterate adult residents of the city."

This might result in an outcome as follows.

EXAMPLE B: FUNCTIONS OF THE LIBRARY

    Educational functions to adults and children
        Programs for adults
           Outreach
              Services for functionally illiterate
    Informational functions to adults and children
    Recreational functions to adults and children

FROM FUNCTIONS TO GOALS

Identify the objectives from the planning documents that relate to each activity or service. While writing your statements, you may discover that some categories need to be further divided or combined for clarity. Some services may need to be deleted as not workable categories. Make sure that all activities and services of the library are included within some program category, thus relating to the major functions. Remember that the key issue for separating activities from functions, programs, and services is essentiality. Functions, programs and activities are essential to maintaining the character of the library. Services are not essential. However, the extent of activities may be altered as objectives indicate.

Example of a Goal Statement

A goal statement for the outreach activity might be the following:

> "The library will develop, within this fiscal year, special responses to the identified needs for outreach activities to (1) the aging, (2) the handicapped, and (3) the functionally illiterate adult residents of the city."

This goal statement takes a part of the library's mission statement and gives it focus for the current year. This focus will be further refined by developing objectives, stated in accomplishable and measurable ways. Goals provide the intermediate focus of each activity or service. They are usually applied in a way that will make it possible to develop appropriate objectives. However, goal statements are general in nature and are not stated in measurable terms. Without their objectives, they cannot be evaluated in terms of their accomplishment.

Let's look at the circulation program identified earlier. A goal statement within that program might read:

"Materials will be shelved promptly to provide for maximum accessibility."

As will be seen in the next section, this goal statement can facilitate the development of objectives for activities and services of the circulation program.

The purpose of writing program goals is to interpret the data gathered during the planning process and relate them to the program's response to those needs. The goal can call for the continuation of activities or for changes to address discrepancies that have been identified through the data developed in the planning process.

DEVELOPING OBJECTIVES
TO PROJECT GOALS

Achievability is critical in setting program goals. Within these program goals you then set objectives for the various activities and services. Your payoff is the ease with which each objective can be evaluated. Let's look at this problem from the perspective of the funding board. It is easy to imagine some member saying, "if you want to achieve these goals, we'll give you the needed funds. But we must know what you'll accomplish."

Your first step is to ask yourself a few questions:

> What do you expect each activity and service to accomplish during the budget year?
> What "time lines" for services must you meet?
> What tasks must you complete?
> What quality of service will be acceptable to you?

Writing Objectives

Most objectives are written in a format developed by Robert Mager. In his format, the objective has three parts:

> What are you going to accomplish?
> How are you going to accomplish it?
> How can you tell when you have accomplished it?

As a school librarian, you are called upon to teach students how to use the library, a demand especially frequent at the beginning of the school year. Your objective might be to meet 90 percent of the demand by (a) extending the library's hours during the first month of the school year or (b) organizing a group of library volunteers to lead the classes in order to meet 90 percent of the demand during the first month of the school year. The change in this case is in the "how" of meeting the expected level of accomplishment (figure 11).

Figure 11. Alternatives for Program Budgeting: Instruction

Objectives	Alternative Methods of Achieving Objective	Estimated Cost
1. Meet 90 percent of skills-training demand in first month of school	1A. Train volunteers to teach library skills	1A. None
	1B. Extend library hours during first month of school: 1 hour per day for librarian and clerk for 20 days	1B. Librarian: $14 × 20 = $280 Clerk: $ 4 × 20 = $ 80 Total $360

Let's look at another example. You are evaluating your circulation program's goal to maximize accessibility through prompt shelving of materials. During the past year the employees of several new companies in town have increased the demand on library circulation. These pressures have resulted in two major problems:

Lines at the checkout counter
Piles of unshelved materials

This is an increasing problem you must consider in your program budget for circulation. How are you to proceed?

Formulate an objective to help define what you plan to accomplish, how you plan to accomplish it, and how to tell when it has been accomplished. In this case, your plan is to decrease the delays in checking out and reshelving materials. Using statistics and data collected about your library's performance, you might come up with a number of alternatives (figure 12).

ALTERNATIVES

A: Reschedule your staff according to library performance data.
B: Budget added staff to check out and reshelve materials faster.
C: Ask a library volunteer to check out and reshelve materials.
D: Do nothing about the problem.

Figure 12. Alternatives for Program Budgeting: Circulation

Objectives	Alternative Methods of Achieving Objective	Estimated Cost
1. Reshelve all over-night returns within first three hours of business	1A. Reschedule staff 1B. Add one hour per day of staff time 1C. Use volunteers 1D. Do nothing	1A. None 1B. $1,196 plus benefits 1C. None 1D. None

How will you know when your objectives have been satisfactorily accomplished? How will you evaluate your efforts? You could decide to:

Allow patrons to wait no longer than four minutes in checkout lines.
Reshelve all materials twice each day.
Allow no more than ten items to accumulate.
Reshelve all overnight returns within the first three hours the library is open.
Expect these high levels of performance 90 percent of the time.

Why 90 percent of the time? It would be unrealistic to set a goal of 100 percent if its accomplishment would require all staff to be present all the time. You cannot set a standard too low either, since it might result in criticism of the library management. You must set an *acceptable* level of accomplishment or you might find yourself defending an attempt to accomplish the impossible, which could undermine your credibility and that of your staff, as well as reducing staff morale. Expecting the impossible places staff members in impossible positions and may result in their becoming discouraged and thus less effective.

Evaluating the Alternatives

Alternative A involves no additional cost. Staff reshuffling, however, could present problems in morale. You could reduce the impact of this problem by discussing slack time and work priorities with each of them and involving them in ways to implement this alternative.

Alternative B results in changing the *personnel* and *employee benefits* line items in the circulation minibudget. If the hourly wage is $4.60, the annual cost of adding just one hour a day of staff time would be $1,196 ($4.60 × 260 working days = $1,196). You can determine the number of hours actually needed by reviewing your library performance (so many items reshelved per hour) and comparing this with the average number of items to be reshelved over a two-week period. If employee benefits are required, the appropriate percentage of wages would be applied to the $1,196 and placed in the employee-benefits line item.

Alternative C calls for no additional cost; but someone on your staff will have to recruit and train volunteers. If a volunteer training program doesn't exist, you will have to develop one. Because the turnover of volunteers is expected to be high, you might need to adjust the 90 percent expectation downward.

Alternative D would leave the situation as it is. You might decide that this need is not worth pursuing, given other priorities.

As a manager, you face the decision of assessing the critical nature of the need and probability of implementing one of the alternatives. Your decision is based on the relationship of *cost* to *effectiveness*. That is, are the results worth the costs? Will the difference be significant? Is this difference critical to accomplishment of the objective?

Using our example, you decide to pursue the situation without additional funds, and knowing that volunteers will probably be too demanding of staff time, you call your staff together to work out a reshuffling of assignments. In your judgment, alternative A is the most cost effective way to achieve the objective. It adds no cost to the budget and will be viewed positively by most funding agencies as wise decision making and wise management.

COMPLETING THE FUNCTION BUDGETS

When you have identified objectives for each of the library's activities and services, you can summarize their costs by using a separate sheet for each objective and each activity and service (figure 13).

Occasionally, there is only one legitimate method of achieving an objective; usually, there will be more. Having identified these methods, you will decide which alternatives will provide the most effective and efficient investment of your library's dollars.

Effectiveness is the degree to which you actually accomplish results. Efficiency involves the lowest dollar investment to achieve the results.

Compiling the Minibudgets

Now you are ready to produce the minibudgets. The process is simplified since the cost of each of the most effective alternatives can now be placed on the activity and service summary (figure 13). These are then added to provide the line-item amounts on each line for the program and thence for the final budget sheet for each function.

Figure 13. Individual Activity or Service Budget Sheet

Activity or Service	Objective
Personnel	
Employee benefits	
Travel	
Purchased services	
Supplies	
Books	
. . . . .	

Figure 14. Function Budget Sheet

Items	Programs					
	1	2	3	4	5	--
Personnel						
Employee benefits						
Travel						
Purchased services						
Supplies						
Book						
. . .						
Total						

Ranking Services and Establishing Priorities

Start with prioritizing if you are called upon to do recision budgeting during an operational year. With few changes you have already ranked your library services when you originally developed this budget.

When all the minibudgets have been developed, you are ready to establish priorities, a necessary step because your budget needs will almost always exceed your expected appropriations. When the budget you have summarized at this point exceeds the expected resources, there are at least three options:

1. Make recisions in services
2. Modify the extent to which the essential activities are carried out.
3. Search for additional funds.

Option 1. Remember that services are not essential to maintain the character of the library. So one of the first places to make recisions is among services. First determine the impact reducing or eliminating a service will have on the library community. How significant is the service both politically and functionally? Which are the highest priority services?

When such questions have been answered, check to see if sufficient recisions have been made to bring the budget total in line with anticipated revenues.

Option 2. Ideally, all services would be eliminated to bring the budget down to the necessary level before proceeding to option 2. However, within the socio-political structure of the library this may not be totally feasible. Therefore, the next step in recision would be to study the activities, not with an eye to eliminating them, for to do so would change the library, but to reducing the scope or intensity of the activity. For instance, in the previous example of circulation, it may be necessary to lower expectations of accomplishments.

Option 3. Seek additional funds either within the parent organization or through Exceptional Sources (Chapter 8).

Figure 13 is the summary sheet for each activity or service. The final total figures would be entered by line item on this sheet. Finally, each of these would be placed on a Function Budget Summary Sheet like figure 14 and the line-item totals summed. Since some needs must be placed on more than a one-year time frame, priorities are usually set for activities of subsequent years as well as for the current year. Several operations occur every year, such as administration, circulation, processing, and acquisitions. Others, like the development and construction of a new library, may be partly carried out during any given year. The program objectives, alternatives, and their costs (as developed in figures 11 and 12) will be invaluable tools for this exercise. You can review the objectives and the cost of alternative methods of achievement to determine the most efficient cost tradeoffs (figure 15). The goal is to achieve the maximum library effectiveness with the funds available. To do this:

> Identify those activities without which the library would cease to function.
> List and rank services according to priority.
> Have your library staff make independent rankings.
> Compile and compare the lists.
> Obtain agreement on priority rankings.

Figure 15. Activity/Service Budget with Detailed Objectives

Library Activity or Service	Personnel	Employee Benefits	Travel	Purchased Services	Supplies	Books	. . .	. . .	Objective Total	Program Total
Act/Service										
Objective 1										
Objective 2										
Objective 3										
Objective . . .										
Act/Service										
Objective 1										
Objective 2										
Objective 3										
Objective . . .										
Act/Service										
Objective 1										
Objective . . .										
Line-Item Totals										

Make recisions as necessary
Compile final budget totals.

Figure 14 indicates a final function budget recap sheet. All developmental materials leading to it become back-up documents that will help guide you through the budgeting process and the budget year especially if you face recision budgeting demands during the operational year.

EVALUATING THE PROCESS

The next-to-the-last step of function budgeting is evaluating the process used for developing the minibudgets. Called *process evaluation,* it seeks to answer such questions as:

Are budget-development time lines being met?
Are all elements in the budgeting process being accomplished in an appropriate manner?
Are the necessary people involved in the budgetary process?
Is the scope of the budgeting process adequate to accomplish the expected results?
Are budget data being gathered about the accomplishment of objectives?
Are staff members aware of their part in the budget data gathering?
Are the appropriate forms ready when needed to gather data?
Is the data gathering sufficient for the scope of the objectives?

If any one of these questions is answered contrary to the intent of the objectives, you can make corrections while the process is taking place. For instance, if the time lines for the year are not being met, determine why and adjust either the timing or the process.

EVALUATING RESULTS

The final step is *product evaluation.* In this step, the effectiveness of the budget in contributing to the management of the library is evaluated. It answers questions such as:

Were the objectives accomplished?
How should the information be organized for presentation?
To whom should it be presented?

There is no general formula or chart you can use to summarize the accomplishment of your objectives. Each objective has its own evaluator built into it. For instance, the higher expectations that reshelving will be maintained 90 percent of the time, and 90 percent of the demand for skills training will be met during the first month of school. Data will be gathered and compared to the standards to determine whether the objectives have been accomplished.

If they have, you will have reasons to refer to them in the next budget proposal process. If they have not, you must learn why. Was the standard too high? Was the objective possible? Did other factors interfere with success? Should you renew the objective for another year?

Feed these answers into your planning process as you prepare for next year's budget. If the initial objectives were reasonably well developed and you managed the library well, most of your standards will have been met. If not, use the experience and information as part of next year's budget development to improve your record. When budget recisions are required, they often have a negative impact on planned accomplishments. As you compile the accomplishments of the year, make sure to indicate this impact. Developing the budget and objectives is not easy, but it won't take as long as you may think. As you become more proficient, you will be able to represent your library, its needs, and functions more effectively each year.

MAKING THE MOST OF EVALUATIVE INFORMATION

As a result of both process and product evaluations, the data

Become input to the subsequent year's planning cycle.
Help in making calculated changes in activities and services.
Alert funding sources to potential problem areas.
Reassure funding sources about the effective and efficient
    use of funds.

Rarely will you be satisfied that all of your objectives have been written carefully enough or that all of the possible alternatives have been considered. Despite any dissatisfaction, when the budget year begins you will have use for everything you have prepared.

After the first year of function budgeting, it will become easier to budget for the ensuing years because you have established a pattern. You shouldn't have to revise function, program, activity and service categories unless the organization undergoes substantial changes or you find that the first year's categories are inadequate.

The main thing is not to be discouraged, the knowledge gained will help to detect and correct any errors made. You are now ready to prepare *next* year's budget. Remember how budgeting cycles overlap. As you put one budget into practice, you will automatically begin preparing the next one.

SUMMARIZING THE PROCESS

Let's summarize the process of function budgeting (figure 16).

Assess needs and planning. Described in chapter 2, this activity establishes the data base for detailing the function budget. It is the reference source of information that leads to the goals and objectives for each identified activity and service area.

Identify functions, programs, activities and services. This process establishes the scope of library activities and the closely related groupings of these activities, providing the framework for budgeting.

Develop goals and objectives. Each category has purposes. The goals and objectives detail these purposes and the actions that will accomplish them.

Develop alternatives. Most objectives can be accomplished in several ways, and alternatives provide a basis for identifying the money to be spent to accomplish them.

Identify costs for each alternative. Identifying costs provides the building blocks of the function budget process. Details are critical at this level. Analyze effectiveness of each alternative. You, as library manager, must decide the extent to which the

Figure 16. The Process of Function Budgeting

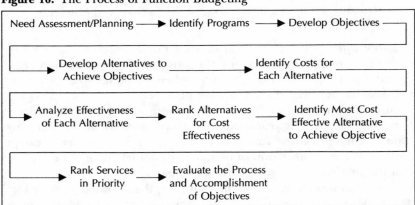

various alternatives will accomplish the objectives. As you gain experience in managing, this task becomes somewhat easier.

Rank alternatives for cost effectiveness. Your professional judgment and knowledge of the organization are important here. You decide, given the costs of the alternatives and the extent to which the objective will be accomplished by each, which alternative has the best "balance" between investment of resources and getting the job done.

Identify the most cost effective alternative. After the alternatives are ranked, the final step is to place the best one on the worksheet for inclusion in the budget for a specific activity or service.

Rank the services in priority. Rank the services in order of their significance in assisting the library to achieve its overall roles in the community, from the most critically important to the least significant. This step also requires weighing their political significance.

Evaluate the process and the accomplishment of objectives. The final step in the function budgeting cycle is to evaluate what has been accomplished. Look to the standards established in each objective in each activity or service and evaluate the levels of accomplishment. Feed this information into your planning system for the subsequent fiscal year.

THE ADVANTAGES OF FUNCTION BUDGETING

Function budgets offer an excellent management tool. With them,

You can evaluate your achievements, since costs are tied to results. (For instance, if your objective is to increase your collection by 5 percent, the cost is related to the increase in the minibudget for acquisitions.) Function budgets require that you identify expected results of activities and services and the format of the process simplifies evaluation.

You can direct and control your operation with ease. Activities and services define specific uses of funds. Therefore, you can change priorities and objectives quickly and easily in the face of budgetary adjustments. Therefore, you can more easily evaluate what should be supported in the face of demands for budget recision.

You work with manageable budgeting units. It is often difficult to conceptualize and analyze the changing needs of the entire library, but not so difficult to analyze the changing needs of smaller units. The latter become the blocks from which the total budget is built. A description of library functions is obtained. The format requires that funds be identified with the functions of the library.

Function budgets make the elements of line-item budgeting simple. Each minibudget maintains line-item identification of funds. Therefore, even the line-item budget becomes more manageable.

Concurrance on the goals and objectives occurs during the budgeting process. Fewer misunderstandings about purpose result when funding boards understand what services they are supporting.

If your plans have been effective, you can monitor the progress of the library. You will be able to answer the funding board member who asks: "What will you accomplish through your efforts?"

EXAMPLE OF FUNCTION BUDGETING IN ACTION

Now that you have studied the processes in function budgeting, let's look at how they could be applied in a real situation. This will help as you design applications in your library (and as you work the assignments at the end of this chapter).

Several approaches to function budgeting in this example illustrate that there are no "right" or "wrong" ways to develop the budget. Sometimes a simpler solution is advisable, and sometimes a more complex approach is called for. The question is whether the resulting budget, which is to be proposed to and approved by the parent organization, is effective. That can never be fully known until approval is obtained and the budget is expended during the operational year.

The Setting

Midtown's population is 50,000. It has a central library of 100,000 volumes, serviced by a staff of 13: 7 professional librarians, 1 custodian, and 5 full-time clerical personnel. Two of the professional librarians are reference librarians. The library budget for the current year is $380,000. Library hours are 9 a.m. to 9 p.m. weekdays, 9 a.m. to 5 p.m. Saturday, and noon to 5 p.m. Sunday. Circulation is 2,000 items a week. The library is equipped with a microfiche reader, a microfilm reader, a copy machine, a record and cassette player, a record and cassette collection,

OCLC and automated card index systems for both serials and books. Ten percent of the population of Midtown are registered library borrowers.

Activities of the library include an extensive children's activity, an interlibrary loan activity, and outreach service in different parts of the city: deposit collection, services for senior citizens, services at a retarded young adults' center, and an adult literacy service.

The town is beginning to experience growing pains in the form of 10 percent growth in the past five years. Two large industries have relocated plants into the area and over a five-year period have added significantly to the population by providing 1,000 new jobs. Now there are rumors of possible layoffs due to the economy.

The library has several problems that need to be addressed in planning and budgeting for the subsequent year. The two reference librarians have seen a substantial reduction in usage and now handle only about twenty inquiries per week. The new industries have made it known that they expected trade journals and reference materials to be provided that relate to their special focus and are of particular interest to their employees. Over the past several years they have provided some funding to assist the library in meeting these expectations.

The young family population has shifted from the traditional south side to the new housing being developed outside the town limits on the north side. Elderly population concentration is increasing due to development of a major retirement village in the old southside community, where urban renewal funds have been used extensively by the town council.

The library is operated as a subunit of the municipality of Midtown and must present its needs each year, along with the other agencies of the town government: the hospital, parks and recreation, police and fire departments, municipal courts, city utilities, the road department, and so forth. The Midtown mayor has indicated that all agencies of town government can anticipate reductions in their next year's budgets. The figure being discussed with the town council is 5 percent.

Applying the Example

For this example, we assume the following conceptualization of a part of the library:

    Public Service
      Circulation
        Outreach
          Senior Citizens
          Retarded Young Adults
          Adult Literacy

This, of course, is a simplified way of identifying the functions, programs, activities and services. Initially, as you work with function budgets, it is well to keep it simple. Obviously, there are many more functions and programs that have additional activities and services.

Outreach as a Single Activity

In outreach, each of the special services could be separated and so budgeted. Or they could all be budgeted together under the outreach label. The decision is usually determined by how they are managed: if together, in a single structure, they are budgeted as a single activity; if separate, they are budgeted separately. In this case, due to the size of the library operation and its management, it has been decided to budget them together.

After we have identified the activities, the next step is to identify the objectives. The goal of outreach in this example is to extend the services and activities of the library into the community to make these services and activities more accessible to library patrons.

The objectives could include the following:

1. Sustain current year's service level of outreach activity through the new budget year by providing the same staffing and operating levels.
2. Meet half of the demand for technical books and periodicals expected by the technical industry employees.
3. Establish a circulation center at the senior citizens' complex not later than December 1.
4. Conduct a needs assessment of persons at the Retarded Young Adult Center by January 30.
5. Analyze demographic characteristics of participants in the adult literacy program by conducting a voluntary survey of the first fall-class meetings. The results will be compared with the current program to determine appropriateness of location and times.

Notice that these objectives are written in a form to simplify their evaluation. Objectives 1, 3, 4, and 5 are evaluated by accomplishing the stated tasks (i.e., Has the same level of staffing and operation been sustained? Was a circulation center established not later than December 1? Was the needs assessment conducted and completed by January 30? Was the analysis of demographic characteristics carried out and the comparison accomplished?) For objective 2, the demand could be met through interlibrary loans. An analysis of the effectiveness of this process would include timeliness and availability of materials. This would establish the extent to which the demand had been met. These represent major objectives for the outreach activity and suggest that the outreach activity is spread among various areas. A baseline is provided through objective 1, indicating that this year's level of service has been satisfactory. If this were the first year to have activity objectives, a rather complete description of services (spelled out through such objectives) would have to be developed. It is usually more effective to keep these in broader (rather than narrower) scope to cover the major purposes for which the activities exist; otherwise a large number of objectives would result, and the sheer weight of them would become oppressive and unmanageable.

For instance, an objective for the previous year might have been "establish contact with the Retarded Young Adult Center to determine if its library needs are being met." The "contact" could be in the form of a luncheon with the director, to establish rapport, and a subsequent visit to the home. This year's objective 4 would then be logical. However, objective 1 indicates that current activities will be continued, including the luncheon with the director and visits.

According to figure 16, the next steps are to

Develop Alternatives to → Identify Costs for
Achieve Objectives   Each Alternative

Thus two items in your budgeting documentation might look like figure 17.

The next steps in the process are:

Analyze Effectiveness   Rank Alternatives for   Identify Most Cost
         of   →   Cost   → Effective Alternative
Each Alternative   Effectiveness   to Achieve Objective

For objective 2, you would proceed as follows. The cost for alternative A is predicted to be $300, to cover postage. (You have estimated that the additional daily burden on the staff will not be noticeable.) The cost of alternative C would be 1/2 hour per day of clerical time plus benefits, and approximately $1,000 for acquisition. Alternative B costs the same as A, the difference being in how the objective might best be accomplished. This depends on the supply of technical books in the state library and the feasibility of establishing an agreement with the technical school.

Figure 17. Listing Alternatives for an Outreach Service

Objectives	Alternative Methods of Achieving Objective	Estimated Cost
1. To sustain current year's level of service of outreach activity center through new budget year by providing same staffing and operating levels	1A. Maintain staffing at same level 1B. No alternative is available*	1Ai. Personnel same, plus 7% raise ii. Employee benefits same, plus 7% raise iii. Supplies same, plus 10% inflation iv. Books/supplies same v. Equipment same
2. To meet half of demand for technical books and periodicals by new-industry residents	2A. Initiate reciprocal borrowing program with a technical-vocational school 2B. Increase state library interlibrary loan 2C. Purchase additional books for collection (Transfer to acquisitions activity center if this is preferred alternative)	2Ai. Personnel same ii. Employee benefits same iii. Supplies (postage) will increase $300 iv. Book/periodicals same v. Equipment same 2B. Same as 2A costs 2Ci. Personnel increase 1/2 hr. per day, clerical time ii. Employee benefits change to cover 1/2 hr. per day clerical time iii. Supplies same iv. Books/periodicals increase by 50 at $20 each v. Equipment same

*This sometimes happens. The objective was stated in such a way as to provide for no alternatives

Nothing would prevent you from adopting both of these alternatives, if both could be worked out. Your initial reaction to the comparison of "A" and "C" is that "A" is more cost effective than "C". However, a key issue is whether this is true only in the short run, or would it also be true in the long run.

Let's look at the long-run economics (figure 18), using a five-year period of time (on the assumption that within 5 years materials in a technical field have changed sufficiently to require repurchase). Thus, it appears that alternative "A" is meeting the objective.

Figure 18. Long-Run (5-Year) Economic Projection

Cost of Alternative A		Cost of Alternative C	
1st year	$ 300	1st year	$1,000 book acquisitions
2nd year	300		½ hr. per day @ $4.60/hr
3rd year	300		× 260 days/year = $598
4th year	300		+ 20% employee benefits
5th year	300		= $119.60
Total	$1,500	Total	$1,718
		2nd year	0
		3rd year	0
		4th year	0
		5th year	0
		Total	$1,718

Perhaps there are other factors to be considered.

1. What is the merit of having the books in the collection, as opposed to the delay in interlibrary loans?
2. Can technical books be obtained through interlibrary loan agreements with either the state library or a technical school?
3. Would purchased technical books go out of date quickly (due to changes in technology), resulting in the need to repurchase before the end of the five-year period?
4. Is expenditure for acquisitions justified by the numbers of potential clientele?

Your answers to these (and other) questions may provide pertinent issues to consider in making your decisions about the benefits of cost efficiency compared with overall effectiveness. You may determine that technical books indeed go out of date quickly due to advances in a field.

You also discover that the cost of such books is at least 50 percent higher than other books you usually acquire. Additionally, you determine that a nearby technical school keeps current on such materials and that its collection could become available to you through an interlibrary agreement. Therefore, the final columns of your document should be as shown in figure 19.

Figure 19. Cost versus Effectiveness Comparison

	Cost Ranking (#1 Least Costly)	Overall Effectiveness (#1 Best)
Alternative 2A	1	1
Alternative 2B	1	2
Alternative 2C	3	3
Alternative 2A is included for placement on your program sheet.		

Each of the other objectives listed for the activity would be extended in the same way. The packages would be summarized on a budget sheet, similar to figure 20.

Figure 20. Activity Budget Sheet Summary

	Current Year	Proposed Next Year
Personnel	$XX.XX	same
Employee benefits	$XX.XX	same
Supplies	$XX.XX	$300
Books/periodicals	$XX.XX	same
Equipment	$XX.XX	same

Each of these budget sheets would be totaled (like the budget sheet in figure 14).

A summary line-item program budget sheet (like figure 15) would finalize the total costs of the library budget and you would then be ready to prepare for budget presentation. With the information you have in hand, you have an in-depth perspective on the proposed operation of your library. You can present, answer questions, and defend expenditure proposals because you know your budget.

PRACTICE EXPERIENCES

1. Develop a chart (like the one in example A, page 39 for your library or for the Midtown library example on page 54. Make sure that all major activities and services are included.

2. For one of the activity or service categories on that chart, develop figure 14 as completely as you can.

3. Design a process and product evaluation process for this category (which you chose in 2 above).

4. Explain how figure 15 would help you and your library when you face recision budgeting demands.

5. Develop your own chart that lists all of the functions, programs, activities and services of a library.

6. Using the chart developed in 5 above, rank order your services from the least critical to the most critical, to form your own priority list of services.

7. Define, in your own words, process and product evaluation.

SELECTED READINGS

Bennett, F. Lawrence. *Critical Path Precedence Networks*. New York: Van Nostrand Reinhold, 1977.

Bittel, Lester R., ed. *Encyclopedia of Professional Management*. New York: McGraw-Hill, 1979.

Bloom, Benjamin S., et al. *Taxonomy of Educational Objectives: Handbook I: Cognitive Domain*. New York: Longman, 1977.

Krathwohl, David R. "Stating Objectives Appropriately for Program, for Curriculum, and for Instructional Materials Development." *Journal of Teacher Education* (March 1965), pp. 83–92.

———, ed. *Taxonomy of Educational Objectives: Handbook II: Affective Domain*. New York: Longman, 1969.

Lee, Sul H., ed. *Planning-Programming-Budgeting System (PPBS) Implications for Library Management*. Ann Arbor: Pierian, 1973.

Mager, Robert. *Goal Anaylysis*. Belmont, Calif.: Pitman, 1972.

———, *Preparing Instruction Objectives*. 2nd ed. Belmont, Calif., Pitman, 1975.

McClure, Charles R., et al. *Planning for Library Services*. New York: Hawthorne Press, 1982.

McConkey, Dale D. *How to Manage by Results*. 3rd ed. New York: American Management Assn., 1976.

Van House, Nancy A., Mary Jo Lynch, Charles R. McClure, Douglas Zweizig and Eleanor Jo Roger. *Output Measures for Public Libraries*. Second edition. Chicago: American Library Association, 1987.

5
Zero Base Budgeting

Use of the planning technique known as *zero base budgeting* (ZBB) is less common now than it was during the early 1970s, an era of "sunshine" legislation, when laws appropriating government funds often required that the funded organizations justify their programs (and even their existence) at the end of each fiscal year. However, ZBB has useful elements for recision situations; so we include the following brief description.

ZBB requires that the cost of all activities and services, both current and new, be justified at the beginning of each budgetary cycle. The justification process demands that administrators look for "creative" ways of solving problems or delivering services, that the alternatives be costed out and then decisions be reached. It requires that the administrator look for services and activities of the library that can be offered at funding levels below the current one, at the current level, and at some prescribed amount above the current level. The resulting packages are then arranged in priority order, from top to bottom, with their costs. At the point where expected or actual funds run out, activities and services below the line are dropped entirely.

MIGHT ZBB BE USEFUL TO YOU?

A systematic appraisal of the strengths and weaknesses of the budgeting process is the first step in deciding whether ZBB will be useful. If the existing budget is well controlled and provides all the data needed to make decisions, you need not apply ZBB techniques. If your budget is expanding, you may not find ZBB critically important. If your organization is so small and limited in funding that cutting would eliminate the organization, you need not apply ZBB. But if you administer an organization that is funded beyond its bare-existence level, if you are in a recision budgetary situation, and if you do not have objective data to help you make decisions, ZBB may be able to help you.

If you decide that ZBB will be useful, you should be clear about your expectations and you should know for whom the information will be generated. The design of the process depends on its consumer.

DECISION UNITS

The first step in implementing ZBB is to define the decision units: a function, program, activity or service, organizational unit, or even a line item or appropriation item. The key consideration is that the decision unit parallel the responsibility for budgetary decision making within the organization. It should be the smallest organizational level possible, managed by someone who uses budgetary discretion.

Your organizational structure will help determine the decision units. Possible decision units in a public library (with branches) or in a school system are the following:

Each library. If each library has a manager who is responsible for resource allocation, the individual libraries may be selected as decision units.

Each activity or service in each library. If the manager of each activity or service in each library is responsible for resource allocation, each activity or service may be selected as a decision unit.

Each activity or service shared by all libraries. If budgetary decisions about library activities and services are made system wide by identifiable managers at the main library, the activities and services shared by libraries may be logical decision units.

The entire library. This may make sense if the library is small and resource allocation decisions are made by the executive officer. This may be the case in a school and in a small public library with no branches.

Besides the size of the organization, another consideration is availability of data. For example, a school librarian may have no more information about library costs than the amount allocated for materials or personnel. If this is the case, preparing decision packages on the library as a decision unit would be next to impossible. ZBB also requires quantifiable performance data. Decision units should be chosen so that each unit's impact is measureable; therefore, unmeasured operations must be included in a decision unit that has a measurable impact.

ASSIGNING COSTS AND BENEFITS

In the initial justification of the decision unit, the manager should first ask if it is necessary and whether its costs outweigh its benefits. To answer these questions honestly, the manager must assign costs and benefits to all of the library's operations. (For example, a circulation decision unit in a public library may cost $25,750, and figure 21 is a hypothetical breakdown.)

After the costs have been determined, benefits must be addressed and this is where work load or performance measures are necessary. Performance measures for the sample circulation decision unit may be as follows:

> Number of circulations per week
> Number of books returned each week
> Number of books to be reshelved from desks and tabletops
> Number of newly cataloged titles to be shelved each week
> Lag between the return of a book and its return to shelf
> Accuracy in shelving
> Number of interlibrary loans requested
> Number of interlibrary loan requests filled
> Number of materials reserved and number picked up after notification
> Number of requests to deliver materials by mail

Figure 21. Decision Unit for Zero Base Budgeting

Shelving	$ 4,000	.5 FTE
Checking out of receiving books	8,000	1.0 FTE
	750	supplies
Overdue notices	1,000	.125 FTE
	330	Postage
	150	envelopes
Interlibrary loan	3,000	.375 FTE
	470	postage
	50	copying
Reserve service, in-house	3,000	.375 FTE
Reserve service, delivery	3,000	.375 FTE
	2,000	postage
TOTAL	$25,750	2.75 FTE

Number of overdue notices
Number of responses to overdue notices
Amount of fines collected
Hours library is open per week.

Someone must decide whether the results are worth their cost. In other words, the judgment must be made that, for $4,000, x books can be shelved a week; for $2,000, $1/2x$ will be shelved, etc. To justify the decision unit the manager must also ask if it can be eliminated. If so,

To what extent is it essential to the library (Chapter 4)?
What would the consequences be?
How many ways can the decision unit's objectives be accomplished?
Which is the most effective way?
How can the efficiency of the decision unit's operation be improved?
What levels of services and costs are possible?

DECISION PACKAGES

After the decision unit is divided into a discrete set of operations, or expenditure items, they "translate" into decision packages. There is no single, right way of presenting decision packages. The form or format is designed to meet the needs of the organization and the expectations of the administrator. It might require such information as:

Purpose
  How accomplished
  Alternatives
  Impact (both positive and negative)
  Accomplishments/workload measures

      or

Statement of purposes
  Description of actions
  Achievements from actions
  Consequences of not approving actions
  Quantitative package measure

      or

Benefits
  Receivers of benefits
  Consequences of not approving package

Consequences of approvng 1/3 of package
Consequences of approving 2/3 of package
Alternatives.

No matter how they are worded, the same questions are posed by each form.

The first package to be put together is the base package, which addresses the essential activities performed by the decision unit. This is viewed as the minimum funding level, below which the decision unit could not exist.

In the circulation decision unit, the head of circulation might see checking out, returning, and shelving materials as the minimum activity level. This represents, according to our figures, $12,750 and 1.5 FTE staff. On a form, he or she is asked to outline:

The benefits of the package
Who receives them
The consequences of not funding the package
Alternative ways of providing the service
The positive and negative impacts of each.

An alternative way of shelving books may be to hire high school students as pages, rather than pay a half-time employee. The advantage would be the low hourly rate. Disadvantages may be the staff time spent hiring, supervising, and training a high-turnover employee pool.

The second decision package (and succeeding packages) addresses only the increase from the previous package. In this case, the second package includes the next highest priority item, which might be interlibrary loan. This represents an additional $3,520 and .375 FTE staff. The total is now up to $16,270 and 1.875 FTE.

The third decision package may be reserve service, which will raise the cost an additional $3,000 and .375 FTE. The total is now $19,270 and 2.25 FTE.

A fourth decision package might be delivery service, amounting to an additional $5,000 and .375 FTE.

The fifth package, overdue notices, amounts to $1,480 and .125 FTE. This brings the funding and staffing to its current level: $25,750 with 2.75 FTE staff.

The current funding level is the same as last year's. It does not take inflation or increased salaries into account. Therefore, it directs itself to the current-dollar level, not the current level of service. If required, a sixth package might be prepared that would reflect the predicted additional cost to maintain the current operational level.

THE DECISION

Usually, no fewer than three decision packages are prepared and seldom more than ten. The same questions about costs and consequences are asked (in narrative form) for each decision package. The head of circulation orders the packages according to his or her priority (see figure 22).

Figure 22. Decision Unit with Ranked Decision Packages

Priority Order	Circulation	Cost	Staff	Cumulative Cost	Staff
1	Circulation and shelving	$12,750	1.5	$12,750	1.5
2	Interlibrary loan	3,520	.375	16,270	1.875
3	Reserve	3,000	.375	19,270	2.25
4	Delivery service	5,000	.375	24,270	2.625
5	Overdue notices	1,480	.125	25,750	2.75

These packages are then sent to you, the director, who receives decision packages from each decision unit of the library. These packages provide a great deal of information on which to base your ranking. In this example, you may recognize that depriving the city of revenue from fines for overdue materials would be politically unwise. You therefore choose to change the order, put package 4 last and recompute the cumulative costs (figure 23).

If you need to recover 20 percent of the decision unit's budget, you may rank the package according to a funding cutoff line. ZBB is not only a tool

Figure 23. The Cut Line

Priority Order	Cumulative Cost	Outcome
1	$12,750 plus	Fundable
2	16,270	Fundable
3	19,270	Fundable
5	20,750	Funding line
4	25,750	Not fundable

to justify budget requests it is also a resource allocation tool. If, after appropriations have been made to the library, the union negotiates salaries that cannot be supported by the appropriation, previously prepared decision packages can help you (or another administrator) pinpoint the operations that will be discontinued to provide the needed money.

SUBSEQUENT YEARS

Will the ZBB approach be as useful to you in subsequent years as during the first year? Clearly, once the decision units and decision packages are defined, they need not change unless circumstances change. In addition, the base need not be justified year after year. ZBB as a management tool can be adjusted to the needs of the moment.

PRACTICE EXPERIENCES

1. From the various ways that decision units can be identified, choose the most effective way to delineate decision units in your library, and set them on paper.
2. Choose one of the decision units just identified, cost it out, and prepare decision packages: one at 80 percent of the current funding level, one at the current funding level, and the third at 110 percent of the current level. Use the form provided, for this exercise and fill it out completely.
3. If you are not in a library situation, use the form provided and prepare a hypothetical justification for each of the five decision packages in the example in the text.
4. Without looking at the text, write a description of the ZBB process.
5. Note ZBB's five advantages as a management tool.
6. Justify ZBB's usefulness in your library situation.

SELECTED READINGS

Cheek, Logan. *Zero Base Budgeting Comes of Age.* New York: AMACOM, 1977.
Chen, Ching-chih. *Quantitative Measurements and Dynamic Library Service.* Phoenix: Oryx Pr., 1980.
———, *Zero Base Budgeting in Library Management: A Manual For Librarians.* Phoenix: Oryz Pr., 1980.
Koenig, Michael E. D., and Victor Alperin. "ZBB and PPBS: What's Left Now That the Trendiness Has Gone?" *Drexel Library Quarterly 21,* (Summer), 1985.

6
Revenue Projections

HOW DO I GET MY FAIR SHARE?

"How can I possibly make a realistic budget request when I don't have any idea how much money they'll give me?" asked one library director. The others in the room nodded their heads in sympathy. "I know I need to start planning earlier," she added, "but I can't wrangle enough information out of anyone until it's too late. And then I have to hurry. It's so frustrating. I'd like to involve my staff and really get things organized for the budget, but with all the rush I just never seem to get there."

A library's building, staffing level, and functions depend on money and timely information. Whereas your goals may be expansive in fat times and moderate in lean times, they must be recisionary in tight money times. Although it never hurts to dream about the possibilities inherent in libraries, your time and energy will be best spent if you are realistic about the activities and services *possible* money can buy. A realistic assessment of revenues is a practical starting point for planning expenditures.

This chapter will provide some answers to various questions you might ask about revenue projection.

> What methods can I use to project revenues?
> What limits should I use in predicting increases or decreases in available funds?
> How can I give my staff appropriate guidelines?
> How can I identify and use an informal communication network?
> What happens if revenue projections are wrong?
> Is it possible to transfer funds from one line item to another?
> Should I count on endowment funds and/or special grant monies?

69

These are not easy questions to answer, and the answers probably will not be the same from year to year. In this chapter you will learn practical ways to reduce some of the unknowns in the revenue projection process.

Budget guidelines, provided formally by the parent organization, usually include such items as percentage adjustments for salaries; adjustments in employee benefits due to changes in retirement costs, insurance, and the like; travel restrictions or increases; or adjustments allowable for utilities. These are usually provided for all units of the parent organization and form some of the formal limits on the development of your revenue projections. Often such guidelines are stated in terms of percentage increases or decreases for the entire budget and/or various line items individually. These must be used in computing revenue projections by each unit, including the library.

DECREASE FRUSTRATION BY RECOGNIZING REALITY

It is less frustrating to plan the activities and services of your library and the expenditure of your budget after you have projected revenues. If, for example, you know that you will be allowed no additional staff, supplies will be increased by no more than 2 percent, and your acquisitions budget will be increased by 20 percent, your thinking may go along these lines.

> Twenty percent increase in the acquisitions budget will allow me to purchase an average of x more titles next year.
> Can my technical services staff process those extra titles in a timely manner? Our goal of titles processed per week may have to be changed.
> Will we be able to absorb the extra cost involved in catalog cards, OCLC terminal time, binding supplies, book pockets and book cards?
> Will the circulation staff be able to shelve the new materials? Will there be space? We might have to weed the collection to free up space.

The answers to these questions may lead you to think about the types of materials on which you will spend the money.

> If we buy reference materials, periodicals, or science books, we will buy fewer titles for the money and will not need to weed the collection. We also will not need more supplies or staff time.
> If we do that, we have made a commitment to continue subscriptions to keep the collection current.

It might be better to spend the 20 percent on more expensive items, like computer software.

Compare the plans you just made to expend a 20 percent increase to those you would make if you face no more than a 3 percent increase in the acquisitions budget.

The purchasing power will be less than this year; so we will be buying fewer titles.

This will free technical services staff time and some library supply money.

Maybe I should approach the Friends of the Library for more software. In fact, I think I'd better take a good look at the library's endowment funds to see if they can be used for additional software.

As you can see, varying revenue projections can send you in quite different planning directions. It is imperative that you learn, as early as possible, what funding level you can expect.

WHOM TO TALK TO

Budget decision makers begin predicting the availability of future funds soon after the current budget has been placed in operation. They study economic, demographic, and funding trends, as well as expected demands from their organizational units. Part of your success lies in your ability to analyze the "who" and the "how" in your parent organization and in the governmental unit with which appropriations are negotiated. You need to find out how their predictions will affect you.

Some people throw up their hands in despair when faced with this question, since they can't count on timely information from the formal system. The formal communication system represents that which can be published through memoranda, house organs, or newspapers. Since this information cannot be disseminated in written form until nearly all uncertainties are resolved, it is not timely in terms of helping you make projections far enough in advance to do adequate budget planning.

For example, no formal announcements can be made about legislative appropriations before the votes are cast. Assume the state legislature meets in March, and your budget must be presented by April for review, with approval in June as a part of your parent organization's overall budget. If you were to await word from the formal system, you would have, at the most, one month in which to calculate the activities and services to support with your projected revenue.

The formal budgeting system can be considered "for the record." It releases budget guidelines for projecting revenues *once* a year; it requests written and oral budget presentations *once* a year; and the decision makers appropriate funds *once* a year. A once-a-year presentation is not enough to convince or educate funding boards on your needs and service capabilities.

This is why the informal communication system is a far more effective route. You need both timely information and frequent access to the decision makers. They need to hear about the library, its operations and needs, more than once a year. The informal network speculates about revenues, levels of program support, priorities for funding, indeed almost any subject that can become a foundation for good budgeting. If you can become a part of this speculation, sharing information about the library and its needs, goals and objectives, your own goals for the library may become more easily communicated and accepted. This can be carried out throughout the year rather than just as part of the final, formal system input.

The "In" Crowd

You can identify and tap into the informal network by approaching people who are at your level on the formal organization chart. Is there a budget analyst with whom you might have coffee? Or an administrative assistant who is "in the know"? During casual conversation, get answers to some very important questions:

> What is the decision-making flow within the organization?
>
> Who makes fiscal predictions and writes budget guidelines?
>
> Who else is involved in the informal system?
>
> Who are the power brokers responsible for tradeoffs from line item to line item and/or from one organizational subunit to another?
>
> What guidelines are being informally discussed? Which ones have changed since last week, or yesterday?
>
> Who are significant advisors to the decision makers? These advisors are often part of both the power-broker group and the informal system. Since they are less visible and vulnerable than the formally identified decision makers, they are often more accessible.
>
> How are budget requests heard in the organization? The formal process is one thing, but the informal information and review system augments your effectiveness in obtaining funds for the library. If you can discuss your revenue needs informally, and early in the year, you will more likely be heard during the formal process.

WORKING FROM THE OUTSIDE

How will "working from the outside" help you with revenue projections? Most organizations develop budgets and budget guidelines through at least two major interactions. The first is internal and the second is external. External interaction includes discussions with governmental units from which major funding commitments are obtained. These can be the state or federal government and/or their regulatory agencies. You should fit them into your organizational chart too.

Governmental units often place limits (guidelines) on the allocation of revenues for subsequent years very early in the budget cycle (which they do not make public until much later), but you need to know what they are as early as possible. So listen carefully to your contacts.

> "It looks like the salary increase for next year won't be over 7 percent."
>
> "Revenues Office is indicating that overall revenues will be down at least 5 percent next year."
>
> "Since energy costs have gone out of sight, any new money will be dedicated to energy costs."
>
> "This'll be a year of recision, for sure. We'll all be tightening our belts."

Such seemingly casual comments should be taken seriously. Develop more than one contact and get in touch with each one every two months during the first half of the budget year and at least once a month during the last half.

WORKING FROM THE INSIDE

The more obvious interactions in budget revenue projections are within your parent organization. Most money appropriated to the municipality or school is not designated for specific uses. Most of the internal allocation of funds to the library or to line items is discretionary with the local decision makers. They often establish their own priorities, but are careful not to violate those "suggested" by the major governmental sources of funds. This is a phase of revenue planning about which you must be keenly aware.

The more often you are in contact with city or school decision makers, the better. They may be in need of some of your reference services for their presentations. This can be the opportunity for you to make sure that they receive prompt and helpful information thus demonstrating in a very visible way the value of your library operation. Each "informal" visit is then an opportunity to present your views of the library and to "negotiate" library allocations.

How To Put It Together

What can you do to be ready to build a realistic budget?

> Develop a file of the names of your informants, dates of contacts, and the information you received. This will summarize the progression of issues through the year.
>
> At the same time, keep a file of public statements by the formal leaders, both within your parent organization and in the governmental agencies through which general funding is obtained.
>
> Discuss with your staff the information you get (but not your sources; people may stop talking with you unless they remain anonymous).
>
> Prepare a chart that identifies the times at which decisions appear to have been made during the year. When are salary guidelines agreed upon? When are total percentage increases or decreases agreed upon? When are incremental percentages for various line items discussed? This chart will be useful in subsequent years, allowing you to anticipate the focus of discussions and ask questions at appropriate times.
>
> Be prepared for changes, surprises, and shifts in power and decisions. Organizations are dynamic entities, and the paramount issues shift throughout the year. Keeping in touch and expecting change will prepare you to fulfill your responsibilities as a budget maker.

Use the information you get through the informal system and project your revenues early in the budget cycle. Apply the guidelines to your budget categories and see how they look. When, finally, you receive the formal budget guidelines, your proposed expenditures will be reasonable, having been tuned to the realities of the revenue picture throughout the year.

RECALCULATING REVENUE PROJECTIONS

We have said that the budgeting process is dynamic. One of the most unsettling surprises could occur after your budget has been reviewed, approved, and appropriated. You might even be halfway through the fiscal year when the governmental unit from which your funds were appropriated learns that it overestimated its projected revenues. If this happens, you probably will be asked to make a budget recision, that is, cut your budget expenditures for the remainder of the fiscal year and in effect, return funds to the parent organization so that its budget will not exceed actual funds which it now expects to receive.

Let's hypothesize that you have been asked to return 2 percent of your budget. The first question is whether the required 2 percent is calculated on the appropriated budget with which you began the year or on the as yet unexpended portion. Two percent of $410,482 is $8,210 (figure 24). If you have expended half the budget, you will have to recover $8,210 from the remaining $205,241—or 4 percent of the remaining funds. But if you calculate 2 percent of $205,241, you have to recover $4,105. It is obviously worth your while to argue for the latter calculation.

Once that question is settled, you have to analyze the unexpended portion of your budget and decide which programs or line items to decrease. If you are working with a function budget, you and your staff have already ranked the services in order of importance. It would be easier to pick one or two of the lowest-ranking services to delete or cut back. Although reductions in services are undesirable, they can be explained and justified.

A function budget also allows the possibility of identifying a service that is popular with members of the funding board or their families. By ceasing children's story hours or the lunchtime speakers' service, you may persuade board members (through "political" pressure) to leave your budget alone and pursue the $4,105 from other agencies.

If you are working with a line-item budget, it is relatively easy to reduce the remaining budget by 2 percent, but you can never be certain how cutting one line item affects activities and services. (Figure 24 will be used as an example throughout this section.)

You might consider decreasing each fund account by 2 percent. After all, an across-the-board decrease is easy to understand and seems fair to everyone. However, some fund accounts are fairly "fixed" through contractual obligations or personnel you have already employed. While there may be some "extra" money in the 100 series accounts due to personnel changes, that may be the only extra money and unless you want to go through some lay offs, the extra money may not be enough to make the 2 percent cut in that line item.

You then look at capital outlay, and here is an obvious $2,063 to return to the municipality or school system. Although you may regret that you had not ordered all the equipment and furniture you had been authorized to buy, the library won't close without that equipment. And if you had placed all the orders and couldn't rescind them, you might have had to turn to more drastic alternatives.

Figure 24. Sample Line-Item Budget (in dollars)

Account Number	Account Title	Actual Expenditures, FY '91	Actual Expenditures, FY '92	Appropriation, FY '93	Actual Expenditures through Dec. '93	Estimated Expenditures, FY '94	Requested for FY '94
100	Personnel services	259,447	267,231	280,592	140,296	280,592	
300	Materials & supplies	70,611	72,729	76,366	38,396	74,324	
400	Contractual services	45,669	47,034	49,386	25,511	49,386	
500	Lease/purchase	2,000	2,060	2,075	1,038	2,075	
600	Capital outlay	1,826	1,882	2,063	—	0	
Total		379,553	390,936	410,482	205,241	406,377	
100	Personnel services	259,447	267,231	280,592	140,296	280,592	
310	Print materials	60,908	62,736	65,875	31,046	63,883	
320	Nonprint	1,770	1,870	1,914	1,800	1,914	
330	Office	3,272	3,375	3,538	1,500	3,488	
335	Custodial	1,947	2,000	2,160	2,000	2,160	
340	Electrical	1,770	1,775	1,914	1,200	1,914	
345	Plumbing	708	730	765	650	765	
350	Safety	236	243	200	200	200	
Total		70,611	72,729	76,366	38,396	74,324	

405	Postage	1,104	1,137	1,472	1,472	1,472
410	Telephone	1,922	1,998	2,078	1,039	2,078
415	Light & heat	25,464	26,209	28,239	14,120	28,239
420	Water	295	303	319	160	319
430	Printing	1,123	1,100	1,012	400	1,012
435	Microfilm	1,121	1,208	1,212	1,000	1,212
440	Binding	826	853	891	290	891
445	Auto. maint.	110	110	120	60	120
450	Leased equip.	564	588	612	306	612
455	Bldg. maint.	12,685	13,060	13,018	6,509	13,018
460	Training	354	364	304	100	304
470	Service contracts	101	104	109	55	109
	Total	45,669	47,034	49,386	25,511	49,386
510	Computer	—	—	—	—	—
520	Copy machine	1,200	1,236	1,296	648	1,296
530	Stationwagon	800	824	779	390	779
	Total	2,000	2,060	2,075	1,038	2,075
610	Furniture	—	800	114	0	0
615	Equipment	1,249	441	1,294	0	0
620	AV equip.	577	641	655	0	0
	Total	1,826	1,882	2,063	0	0

You are left with the contractual services and materials and supplies funds. Unless you decrease library hours, your utility bills, leased equipment, service contracts, and building maintenance are unlikely to change—and you have already expended all of your postage money. This leaves printing, microfilming, binding, and training in the contractual services account. The fact is that you can't really anticipate the impact of decreasing those line items.

You finally decide it will be easiest to subtract the remaining $2,042 from the materials and supplies account. You'll buy fewer titles and supplies this year than planned. Because acquisitions represent a large percentage of the budget, and the money represents only 3 percent of the print budget, why not? It doesn't seem to make that much difference, in the short run. Miscalculations of revenues are out of your control, but they happen; and the control you have over your budget and its support of activities and services is vitally important. You must be sure it has been designed to provide you with the management data you need in all circumstances. Also, you must be able to look at the long-run effects of budget cuts. In the above example, you cannot be sure what the long-run effect will be from cutting the most meaningful activity you offer.

TRANSFERS AMONG FUNDS

Although line-item budgets are less-than-ideal management tools for preparing budget cuts, they are flexible when you must deal with internal fund transfers. The expenditure of each 300-level line item need not balance what was budgeted as long as the *entire* Materials and Supplies account balances.

For example, if you were to buy computer software from your non-print account (320), you would probably spend more than the appropriated $1,914. That will most likely be unchallenged, as long as the entire Materials and Supplies expenditure balances with its appropriation. It is not as easy to move money from one fund account to another. If you try to buy computer software from your acquisitions budget, your accounting department may return the purchase requisition, thinking software is capital outlay.

To move money from the 320 account to the 615 account, you almost always have to make a special request, justifying the need, at a hearing before the finance board or budget committee. This is not impossible, however; you follow the same thought processes you used when you justified the budget. If you have established your need, considered alternatives and chosen the most sensible one, and can explain it clearly, your request may be honored.

ENDOWMENT FUNDS

"I've always viewed endowment funds as discretionary, special-use funds, but they're hardly worth going after now," a library director complained. "My funding board is asking me to project the income from our endowment funds, and then they'll subtract that amount from their appropriation."

Endowment funds can be very useful, especially during lean times. Ideally, they will not be reflected in the library's budget. You do not want your appropriation to be made with those funds subtracted; you want them to remain separate and discretionary. Each endowment may have various requirements. Some allow you to spend principal and interest; others restrict your spending to interest only. Some specify that they be used only to purchase books, records, or material on a specific subject.

Give some thought to endowments and, through your board and legal counsel, determine the most beneficial way for people to leave money to the library.

> Should money be left to the municipality, or to the school or library board of trustees?
>
> Are you going to plan a recognition program, such as bookplates, plaques, or published lists of donors?
>
> How will you keep track of gifts given in memory of others? How will you answer the stranger who appears ten years from now, asking to see all the purchases bought in her mother's memory?
>
> Will you need a policy that allows you to "weed" outdated purchases? Should potential benefactors be told that this is a possibility?
>
> Do you prefer restricted funds? Restricted funds can be advantageous if, for example, you can spend the money on only one medium (such as live music) or subject (such as target shooting). You may be able to initiate an excellent concert series or build a notable collection that will bring attention to the library.
>
> Do you prefer unrestricted funds? Left to your discretion, these funds can be used to fund experimental services until the need for the program is firmly established and the parent organization is willing to fund it.

It is worth your while to provide information about endowments to your public, making it easy for them to leave money to the library. If you prepare a brochure explaining the procedure, you can suggest ways in which they can state their intent and be sure that they will benefit your activities and services.

In times of recision budgeting these funds need to be studied even more carefully. Is it possible to use some of them to accomplish objectives that have had to be bypassed due to funding cuts? Are there ways to highlight in your public information about endowments, the various areas of library development that probably will not be funded under the regular budget? Carefully developed endowments can allow you to provide unusual or special services. They can also be among your most successful public relations efforts.

SUMMARY

Revenue projections are made before budget preparations; and it is upon expected money that you determine activities and services levels. But the process does not stop there. The revenue picture can change any time during the budget year:

> You may be asked to return an unexpended portion of your appropriation to your funding body.
> You may be "blessed" with a donation (such as a computer) that makes unanticipated demands on other line items.
> Unforeseen price increases could occur during the year for services you are committed to purchase.

These are a few challenges that crop up during the fiscal year. The next chapter continues the process of budget expenditure.

PRACTICE EXPERIENCES

1. Develop an informal organizational chart for your parent organization.

2. Identify at least two informational communication contacts within the fiscal branch of your organization. If you are a student, discuss this issue with a practicing librarian.

3. Develop guidelines for an endowment fund, considering ways of responding to the questions posed in this chapter.

4. Working with the budget in figure 24, identify two more ways to recover $4,105 from the unexpended funds. How could you recover $8,210?

SELECTED READINGS

Dixon, Robert L. *The Executive's Accounting Primer.* 2nd ed. New York: McGraw-Hill, 1982.

Prentice, Ann E. *Public Library Finance.* Chicago: American Library Association, 1977.

Simini, Joseph Peter. *Accounting Made Simple.* New York: Made Simple Books, 1988.

Spiro, Herbert T. *Finance for the Nonfinancial Manager.* 2 ed. New York: Wiley, 1982.

7
Expenditure Projections

Projecting of expenditures is a major step in the preparation of your budget. Chapters 1, 2, 3, and 4 provided the foundation concepts of budget development, and in Chapter 6 you learned about critical issues in projecting revenues. Now you are ready to develop the second part of your budget—the part most people refer to as *the* budget: expenditure projections. This chapter will suggest the most commonly used processes for doing so. However, since it is largely an explanation of the computational processes, you need to keep in mind the previous four chapters mentioned and refer to them often.

For instance, the function information and ranking in the "Practice Experiences" in Chapter 4 will prove invaluable as you compute your budget expenditures in this chapter. The expected levels of revenues projected through application of Chapter 6, provide the foundation for your decisions about expenditures.

The following are major objectives in this chapter:

> Identification of sources of expenditure-projection information
> Description of the significance of expenditure projection in budget development
> Computation of the impact of inflation on expenditures
> Development of a three-year expenditure analysis chart
> Development of a subsequent-year expenditure-projection chart.

HOW MUCH IS ENOUGH?

Projecting budget expenditures is a critical and demanding function, which librarians, as managers, are expected to carry out. As you look forward to each budget year, you will consider many uses for your anticipated revenues. Your major challenge is to make accurate and acceptable projections of expenditures for these programs. To overestimate needed funds may seem to be a comfortable approach; however, *overprojecting* has two effects:

All of the funds might not be used, leaving you vulnerable to *underfunding* the following year.

If the amount of funds for each budget category is inaccurately projected, some categories may not have sufficient funds. Later requests for fund transfers among categories are often considered poor practice by funding agencies. On the other hand, underestimating may leave you struggling to achieve your objectives for the entire budget year, and vulnerable during the next budget request period. It is therefore extremely important to learn to project budget expenditure fully and accurately.

WHAT APPROACH?

Two approaches can be utilized to develop accurate budget projections. They involve looking back at actual expenditures and looking ahead to development of an accurate projection.

How can you look back to extract and use appropriate data and information from previous years' budgets? You should obtain copies of the budgets for the two previous years of operation and for the current year. These budgets should be in your files; if not, they can usually be obtained through your accounting or principal's office. (If you are a student, you may be able to get copies of the library budgets through a school bookkeeper, a city accountant, or your state librarian.) To supplement them and to focus your efforts, you might also read the library's annual reports.

The first step in making projections is to get all the information you can about the uses of budgeted money for the past two years and the current year, that is, how all available revenues for that period were budgeted and used. Remember, you need to get both the approved budget and final budget for each year. The approved budget *authorizes* expenditures while the final budget shows *actual* expenditures. These figures are often different (usually due to line-item transfers or to underspending certain accounts); so both are important to you in making projections.

POSTING

Once you have the data from the past and the current years in hand, you are ready to *post* the comparative budget items. First, make sure that the layout or format for each of the years is the same. The budget categories should match, whether they are line items or function format. If they do not appear to be the same, ask the accounting office or a librarian for assistance in matching expenditure categories for these years. (Changes in nomenclature, which frequently occur in budget formats, do not necessarily reflect actual changes in budget items.) You need to make these determinations before proceeding. For instance, "Contractual Services" as a line category one year may become "Purchased Services" in a subsequent year's budget.

It will be easier to deal with the overall budget figures by line items at first. Later, you may want to construct a function budget chart, as explained in Chapter 4. To post the expenditures, copy figure 25 or develop a similar one of your own. There should be a separate line for each category that has been or will be used in the budgets. Take the approved budget figures for the second year back and place them in the first column on the chart. Place the figures for the next two years in the appropriate columns. Next, take the final or actual budget expenditures for each line-item category and place them in the "final" column for each specific year. This will give you a visual layout of the changes. Next year's projections will be placed in column 8.

However, before you go on to column 8 you must analyze the information you have collected. For each budget line item, compute

> The percent change from the first year back to the second year back. Divide column 5 by column 2, then subtract 1. Enter the result into column 3. If the result is less than 1, place it in parentheses (this represents a reduction in funding).
>
> The percent change from the first year back to the current year. Divide column 8 by column 5, subtract 1, and enter the result in column 6.
>
> The percent change from the second year back to the current year (the total percent change). Divide column 8 by column 2, subtract 1, and enter the result in column 9.

INFLATIONARY IMPACT

Ascertain the national inflation rate for each year. Any increase beyond the inflation rate is probably due to actual growth or change in library programs. Your annual reports should assist you in identifying the reasons for this increase or prices of materials and utilities have grown more quickly than the consumer price index. Make notes on these changes so you will have them readily available as you continue your

Figure 25. Projecting Expenditures from Previous Expenditures

Program: _____

	1 1992 Approved	2 1992 Final	3 1993–92 Final %	4 1993 Approved	5 1993 Final	6 1994–93 Final %	7 1994 Approved	8 1994 Projected Expd.	9 1994– 1992 %
Personnel services									
Librarian	___	___	___	___	___	___	___	___	___
Technical	___	___	___	___	___	___	___	___	___
Custodial	___	___	___	___	___	___	___	___	___
Other (specify)	___	___	___	___	___	___	___	___	___
Benefits									
FICA	___	___	___	___	___	___	___	___	___
PERA	___	___	___	___	___	___	___	___	___
Group insurance	___	___	___	___	___	___	___	___	___
Other (specify)	___	___	___	___	___	___	___	___	___
Matls. & supplies									
Books	___	___	___	___	___	___	___	___	___
Periodicals	___	___	___	___	___	___	___	___	___
AV materials	___	___	___	___	___	___	___	___	___
Office	___	___	___	___	___	___	___	___	___
Custodial	___	___	___	___	___	___	___	___	___
Electrical	___	___	___	___	___	___	___	___	___
Plumbing	___	___	___	___	___	___	___	___	___
Safety	___	___	___	___	___	___	___	___	___

analysis. Ask yourself: Are these activities and services going to continue to increase or decrease for the next year? If so, at the rate indicated from year to year on your chart? Not as much? More? Try to be as realistic as possible. If an activity or service is declining, project the decrease (unless you have a valid reason not to do so).

> Are there services or activities that will demand increases in line items to provide adequate support?
> Are major changes in personnel anticipated that will affect the line-item trends? For example, retirements result in replacement of personnel by less experienced and, therefore, less expensive persons.
> Have there been major shifts in demand on library activities and services that may result in greater (or lesser) fund demands in line items?

As these kinds of questions are posed and answered for each activity and service and each line item, the basis for projecting to the next year's budget expenditure is clarified. Figure 26 will help to organize this information for line items. The information gathered in preparing figure 26 and the notes you have taken are essential in making your projections.

Increases are based on increased demand for activities and services and on the projected impact of inflation on each line item. The impact of inflation may vary from one line item to another. Book prices, for instance, probably will increase at a greater rate than salaries or supplies. Sources of information, like the *Bowker Annual*, will help you establish such projections. Utilities may increase at a greater rate than books. (Your parent organization usually has a *factor* for you to use for utility increases.) As the cost of utilities is projected for each separate library, the resulting information may influence your decisions. For instance, if small branch libraries or school libraries are comparatively expensive to operate, this information may be a basis for closing them or radically altering their hours of operations.

IMPACT OF PROGRAMS AND SERVICES

After you have dealt with inflationary increases, increases in activities and services must be considered. It is at this point that your established objectives become vitally important. As you completed your needs assessment and planning as explained in Chapter 2 and identified your functions, programs, activities and services as discussed in Chapter 4, you identified these objectives. Now, as you begin to project expenditures, your major concern is to provide the necessary support to accomplish those objectives.

Figure 26. Projecting Expenditures for Changing Activities/Services

Activity or Service: _____

	Most Recent Inflation Factor or Price Index	Factor for New or Additional Services	Next Year's Expenditure Projection
Personnel services			
Librarian			
Technical			
Custodial			
Other (specify)			
Benefits			
FICA			
PERA			
Group insurance			
Other (specify)			
Matls. & supplies			
Books			
Periodicals			
AV materials			
Office			
Custodial			
Electrical			
Plumbing			
Safety			
Contractual service			
Postage			
Bldg. maint.			
Training			
Travel			
Postage			
Telephone			
Light & heat			
Water			
Printing			
Lease/purchase			
Capital outlay			
Bldg. improvement			
Equipment			
Furniture			
Other (specify)			

Of course, if the projection of expenditures exceeds the projection of revenues, only two possibilities exist:

Increase proposed revenues.
Reduce proposed expenditures.

The objectives to be accomplished and the services to be provided would be reduced by the latter action. As you may have observed, function budgeting provides an excellent basis for such decisions. Your resulting budget should provide an alignment of objectives and expenditures to achieve these objectives for the subsequent year.

EXPENDITURE ANALYSIS CHART

Completion of figures 25 and 26 is necessary before you proceed with the expenditure-projections process. For example, let's look at a line item for audiovisual materials (figure 27).

Your needs assessment may have identified a major increase in use of AV materials due to the shift from print materials to increasingly available media-based materials. You proceed by computing the percentage of difference from the various years. The second year back to the first year back is an increase of $180 (or 8.1%) in the approved budget and an increase of $252 (or 11.7%) in the final expenditures. The first year back to the current year is an increase of $1,200 (or 50%) in the approved budget and an increase of $1,204 (or 50.2%) from final to projected expenditures. The second year back to the current year is an increase of $1,380 (or 62%) for the approved budget and $1,456 (or 67.9%) from the final to projected expenditures.

Differences between approved budget increases and final budget increases are not critical, unless they are extreme. Extreme increases or

Figure 27. Sample Expenditure Projection: Materials Budget

Materials	1 1992 Approved	2 1992 Final	3 1993– 92 Final %	4 1993 Approved	5 1993 Final	6 1994– 93 Final %	7 1994 Approved	8 1994 Projected Expd.	9 1994– 92 Total % Change
Books									
Periodicals/ newspapers									
AV	$2,220	$2,144	11.7	$2,400	$2,396	50.2	$3,600	$3,600	67.9

decreases need to be taken into account and explained as they relate to projections for the subsequent year. These figures are entered in the appropriate columns in figure 25.

In figure 26, for instance, you may have identified (through your suppliers) an estimated inflation factor of 5 percent for AV materials for next year. You also have identified that you would like to increase your services in this area by approximately 15 percent through the provision of new materials. Therefore, you can project in two ways:

> Divide your column 9 increase by 2 (divide 2) resulting in an overall per year increase of approximately 34 percent, to which you add the 5 percent inflation factor, for a 39 percent total increase.
>
> Or use the estimates of 15 percent for services increase and add the 5 percent inflation factor, for a 20 percent increase.

The results of the first method would be $5,004, and the second method would yield $4,320. Your decision as to which method to use would be based on your assessment of the possibilities of substantiating your request at your budget hearings.

OTHER RESOURCES

To obtain the information to assist you in making these projections, a number of additional sources can be identified and used. The experiences and observations of your staff should be invaluable in making projections. The interaction of the staff may also result in creative approaches to managing expenditures and facilitating goal accomplishment. Suppliers, jobbers, and vendors can be contacted for prices or for estimates of inflationary impact on their products or services. They usually know what the price increase will be in their businesses well in advance of your operational year. You should contact them and obtain this information.

The *Bowker Annual* and articles on U.S. periodical and serial services price indexes, which appear in *Library Journal,* are excellent sources of information for historical price increase trends. The price/cost indexing system for books and serials that they provide will permit you to justify larger-than-inflation increases in your budget and/or to identify accurately the impact that less than adequate funding will have on the library. These sources offer a more reliable cost-projection system for books and serials than using the standard rate of inflation, since they relate specifically to books and serials (rather than *all* goods and services).

For instance, a review of price changes from 1980 to 1990 reveals that periodicals in chemistry increased 240 percent, in engineering and technology 230 percent, in literature and language 226 percent, and in library and information science 227 percent (Harr, p. 486). Increases in excess of the standard rate of inflation should be used in interpreting your budget increases to decision makers in your parent organization.

CHANGES IN EMPHASIS

Decisions about developing the collection are ongoing, but your emphasis may be different from year to year, and this may affect your projected book and serial expenditures. For example, one of your new programs may be to further support the business community by building the business collection. Or the school may be beginning a fine arts program and you are expected to develop an art collection that would support it. The *Bowker Annual* presents a chart of average per volume prices of hardcover books from year to year. It lists subject categories with Dewey Decimal Classification numbers.

In 1991, the average price of a business book was $43.00 and the average price of an art book $45.00. The amounts are meaningful when compared with fiction, which averaged $22.00 per volume (Grannis, p. 503). Therefore, using this example, you might prefer to deemphasize one area of the collection to buy business books from the current year's budget. Buying art materials would certainly require that you project a sizable expenditure for the subsequent year's book budget.

WHAT PERCENT FOR BOOKS, WHAT FOR SERIALS?

If books and serials are on the same line of the budget, you will have to make a conscious decision about the percentage you are willing to spend on each. The increase in costs of serials may require a cutback in serial purchases or a decision to spend ever larger percentages of materials money on periodicals. You may also want to study the impact of a CD ROM package for part of the serials collection. The need to maintain expensive serial titles may not be as strong in a public library as it is in a school, where journal subscriptions are necessary support for curricula. A yearly analysis of the balance between serials and monographs should be a routine part of the projection of expenditures. You, as a manager, can make a reasoned projection that can be included in your budget presentation.

SUMMARY

You must get your city's or institution's guidelines for inflation and acceptable levels of budget increases. In a few areas, such as salaries and benefits, these must be used for projections. In other areas the guidelines are somewhat flexible and are provided to assist you in considering budget changes. When you exceed the guidelines in the flexible areas, you must be prepared to provide descriptions, explanations, and data to assist budget decision makers in understanding the basis for your expenditure projections.

As you work with the projection for each line item, bring all your data together and establish your rationale for the proposed expenditures. This rationale will be the basis for your budget presentation to your library board, your council, or your chief administrator.

PRACTICE EXPERIENCES

1. Complete figure 25.
2. You have been requested to make your subsequent years expenditure projections based on a total of 5 percent recision. Rework your budget per figure 25 in order to comply with this recision figure.
3. Explain how the acquisition of a CD ROM as a part of your serials collection could impact your serials cost.

SELECTED READINGS

Bankhead, Betty. "Through the Technology Maze: Putting CD ROM to Work." *School Library Journal,* Oct. 1991.

Brown, Norman B., and Jane Phillips. "Price Indexes for 1982: U.S. Periodicals and Serial Services." *Library Journal,* pp. 1379–1382 (Aug. 1982).

Dessauer, John P. "Book Industry Markets, 1976–1985." *Book Industry Trends, 1981,* Research Report No. 11. New York: Book Industry Study Group, 1981.

Grannis, Chandler B. "Book Title Output and Average Prices, 1991 Preliminary Figures." *Bowker Annual of Library and Book Trade Information,* 37th ed., pp. 502–508. New York: Bowker, 1992.

Harr, John. "Prices of U.S. and Foreign Published Materials." *Bowker Annual,* 37th ed., pp. 481–502. New York: Bowker, 1992.

8

Exceptional Sources
of Revenue

WHY CONSIDER OTHER REVENUE SOURCES?

Not all the projects planned by your library will be funded. Through your
needs assessment and planning activities, you will almost certainly come
up with more needs than money (Chapter 2). Additionally, when the
function budgets are planned and ranked, some services are excluded
from funding (Chapter 4). As the budget year proceeds, you may
become aware of additional needs for which there are no resources,
unless you were to reallocate funds. Reallocation might be neither
politically wise, in view of your relationship to your funding agency, nor
economically possible, if you are to fulfill the goals and objectives for
which you planned. You are caught in a dilemma: to postpone responding to the additional needs until the next budget year or to pursue other
alternatives. This chapter includes ideas that might help you meet this
new challenge by suggesting *exceptional sources of revenues*—that is, funds
for the exceptions that arise outside your planned operation or that were
not funded by appropriated revenues. The chapter will suggest resources
useful in locating such funds and ideas about some of the critical
questions to be answered in pursuit of such funds.

GETTING THE MONEY

Following are two conversations representing different approaches to
funding sources. In one library, you might hear this conversation:

"I hear they're funding programs for the handicapped this year. Let's get the money for a TTY or some large-print books. That way we'll have more acquisition money for other things."

"That may be a good idea. How many visually impaired people are there in this city?"

"I don't know, but who cares? That's where the money is this year. Let's get our share."

A different discussion may be pursued in another library:

"Some of our elderly patrons have been complaining about the large-print books we bought last year. They're too heavy to hold. What do you think we should do?"

"I understand there are funds available for that sort of thing. Let's look into some of the other large-print publishers and see if we can find something lighter in weight. While we're at it, let's survey our patrons to see if they'd be interested in large-print crossword puzzles.

"In fact, let's see if we can get another library to work with us. We could share resources that way—we can get twice as many titles at half the cost."

"That's a terrific idea. In fact, the LSCA guidelines *recommend* funding for cooperative projects. We can't go wrong."

These are two approaches to seeking exceptional sources of funding. You can identify the kinds of projects that are in vogue at the moment and create a "need" to meet the funding requirements, or you can define your needs and then seek funding.

BEFORE WRITING A PROPOSAL

The need is identified as a part of your regular needs assessment and planning process (Chapter 2). The special need for which you might seek funding may represent a new area of service for the library, or it may be low on your priority list. New areas of service are often difficult to introduce during lean times or when budget recisions are the rule. Low priorities are often areas of need that simply cannot be funded due to the ranking process. Sometimes, however, these needs coincide with special funding interests of the federal or state government.

Occasionally, inquiries from special groups or institutions within your community will call your attention to revenue resources. Or you may become aware of funds through your research into possible sources of grant money. However you become aware of them, you will carefully consider the time involved in both proposal preparation and fund administration. Grant administration often requires more oversight and evaluation than you may wish to spend. But even when these requirements are considered, it may seem to be worthwhile.

IS IT FUNDABLE?

Once you identify an idea or isolate a need, you have to determine whether it is fundable from an exceptional source of revenue. Therefore, study of various reference sources should be a basic part of every librarian's education. (A number of reference sources are described later in this chapter.) It takes hard work to become familiar with sources, but the effort is worthwhile if you develop a grant proposal. Once you are familiar with the references and the possibilities they suggest for funding, the next time a need is identified that cannot be covered with local funding, you will have a good idea whether it might be fundable from a special source and you will know whether to proceed with planning and application.

Except for locating sources of funds and tailoring your proposal to their special requirements, the grant-getting process is a miniature exercise in function budgeting, such as you studied in chapter 4.

STEPS IN THE PROCESS

First, assess the impact of the grant on your institution: its potential positive and negative effects within the organization. For instance, will the library staff be able to process the number of volumes you plan to buy with the money you are seeking? Will your acquisitions budget be cut by the administration because you received a grant, thereby decreasing your appropriated base of funds and decreasing the impact of future percentage increases from regular budget sources? You may want to sound out this dilemma with one of your information contacts within the parent orgnization. If you apply for a grant to allow you the experience of working in another library for several months, will the current staffing level be adequate for the necessary library activities? If so, how will you justify your position, if you can be away six months and there is no negative effect on your library's operation? How will you arrange coverage while you are gone?

Questions of this nature must be asked as part of your initial assessment of the impact of a grant on your institution, before you get into the details of writing the grant proposal. Your assessment of the effects of grant money on the institution should address the impact on staff, activities and services, processes, and regular funding.

Second, perform a needs assessment to be sure that the need you perceive exists and is high among the priorities of the library staff, board, and community (see Chapter 2).

Third, search the literature to discover whether your idea has been tried before and with what results. For instance, has a services "package" for children already been accomplished elsewhere? Has a collection of suitable books for elderly citizens been identified? Are there literacy services that are recommended for library utilization? Do materials exist that describe the significant subcultures in your area? Have other states already developed a shared information base system for archives?

Such services have been funded through exceptional sources of revenues for various libraries across the nation during recent years. When you write your proposal, you will want to cite such services to obtain credibility for your ideas.

Fourth, make sure that the support from your community is identified and included in the proposal. Support may be confirmed by any "hard" or "soft" match of funds required by the grant. However, letters of support are also useful.

Fifth, investigate the various funding sources, select one, and through a telephone inquiry confirm that your idea will interest that source. Then follow the telephone conversation with a letter. When you receive the application form and instructions, write the proposal, directing it at the requirements and expectations of that funding source.

The format of proposals varies among funding sources, but the general information requirement is usually similar (Hillman, 1980). Three issues are critical to funding sources:

> Importance of the problem
> Value of the solution
> Demonstrated ability to carry out the project.

ASK FOR HELP

At this point you need to contact the administration, or the city or town accountant. There may be matching funds or in-kind contributions the library, school, or city will be required to make.

Do not be discouraged if a granting agency requires a hard or soft match. A hard match refers to an equal-dollar amount that is a stipulation of the grant. This is often more difficult to get than a soft match (or in-kind contribution) because it involves the commitment of real money.

It is important to discuss hard-match requirements with your accountant or fiscal manager to determine if hard-match monies are available and whether you can submit such a proposal. Generally, official statement of hard-match availability is needed when the proposal packet is sent to the funding agency.

A soft match is the most common matching requirement. The amount will differ among granting agencies, and "creativity" in defining such contributions is needed on your part. Soft-match ideas include:

> If equipment owned by the library will be used during the project, you can assign a rental fee to it and make this dollar amount your donation to the project.
>
> If you rely on staff to carry out the project, you can declare an appropriate percentage of their salaries in-kind contributions. (This can be applied under some definitions of hard match as well.)
>
> If meetings of an unpaid advisory board are part of your service, the cost of their transportation to those meetings can be declared part of your match.

Your fiscal officers (having prepared grant proposals before) will be able to make many suggestions about meeting the required grant obligations.

PROPOSAL WRITING

Proposals are like the written budget presentation you make to your board every year (Chapter 9). Begin with a description of your library: its location, staff and collection size, and clientele. This "sets the scene" for what follows and suggests that you and your institution are credible. The description could be patterned after that of Midtown library in Chapter 4.

Then present a problem statement that is substantiated by your needs assessment. Be sure to use appropriate statistics, objective facts, and be client centered.

Let's pick a problem from the Midtown example: "The elderly population is increasing due to the development of a major retirement village in the old south-side community." The formulation of the problem could read:

A recent study of population changes in Midtown (conducted with Midtown's continuing urban renewal planning) has identified a 20 percent increase in residents over 60 years of age in the 50-square-block area of the city known as South Side. A major part of this increase has been due to the opening of a "retirement village" in that area. The library has contact with this village and, as a result, has developed a collection of large-print books. However, according to a survey conducted among 100 patrons who use the collection, over 50 percent of the books are too heavy for them to handle comfortably. Additionally, over 60 percent of the residents of the village do not have transportation to the main library where the collection is housed. There is no branch library.

Set forth your objectives, which should be attainable, measurable, timely, and client centered. Follow with your methods or procedures and a justification for choosing these particular plans and resources.

The objectives of your project could be the following:

An agreement with the retirement village for expanded library services at the village center.

A survey to determine the reading interests of the population.

An addition of 100 titles of large-print books for the special collection. These books will represent the interests of readers identified in the survey and will be of a size and weight for easy handling.

Subscriptions to at least 20 periodicals that are identified as of interest to the readers.

A circulation center, in operation in the retirement village not later than December 1.

Hiring residents of the village as part-time circulation staff.

Then, in justification of the project, write something like this:

It is the intent of this project to provide the greatest possible service to the elderly citizens by meeting their identified needs directly. It appears to us that establishing a small collection and circulation center provides a simple answer.

One of our intentions, should this proposal be funded, is to hire part-time assistants from the village to staff the circulation center. Funds are requested for this purpose. Hiring part-time assistants will be less expensive than providing regular library staff. Basic supervision and assistance will be provided through the regular library staff as part of the required match.

The results of this outreach service will be disseminated through a project report provided to your agency six months after establishment of the circulation center. The report will include acquisitions problems and issues, selection of books and periodicals, circulation information, staffing experiences, and other information that would be useful.

Next, identify a "time frame" in which the need will be met, the staff provided (as well as the fiscal agent you will use), and how the results of the program will be disseminated (see figure 28). A Gantt chart (such as this) can identify your methods and procedures clearly and easily. If needed, a description of each item on the chart could be provided in narrative form. This decision is determined by the instructions in the proposal guide you have acquired from the funding agency.

The time lines are identified in figure 28. However, it should be noted in the proposal that if the December opening is to be met, a funding decision is needed not later than June 1. If the decision is later, the opening will be correspondingly later.

A vital part of your proposal is evaluation of the services: both the end product (*product* evaluation) and the methods used to attain it (*process* evaluation). Process evaluation includes procedures that monitor the implementation of a project, such as

Time lines: Are things being done when they were projected?
Data gathering: Are data identified? Are formal procedures initiated so that the data needed at the end of the project will have been gathered?

Figure 28. Gantt Chart for Grant Application

	Apr.	May	June	July	Aug.	Sept.	Oct.	Nov.	Dec.
Agreement	- - -								
Survey		- - -							
Book acquisition			- - - - - - - - - - - - - - - - - -						
Periodical subscription		- - -							
Cataloging					- - - - - - - - - - - - - - - - - -				
Center plans		- -						
Staffing						- - - - - - - - - - - - - -			
Set up						- - - - - - - - - -			
Opening of center									- - -

Procedures: Are procedures developed and carried out that might be expected to lead the project to a successful conclusion?

People issues: Have the appropriate people been involved, hired, and oriented so that the project is facilitated through their efforts?

Fiscal control: Have fiscal control policies and procedures been developed and used?

Remember, the focus of this phase of evaluation is monitoring the process as it takes place.

Product evaluation, the other phase, deals with formal questions that must be answered about the overall effectiveness and efficiency of the project.

Were the purposes (goals and objectives) for which the project was initiated achieved?

Does the public feel the project was worthwhile?

What conclusions do the summary data support?

What has been (should be) done to assure the continuance of services, materials, etc., after the end of the project?

What were the impacts of the project on the organization and on its ability to carry out its mission?

Plan the evaluation process as an integral and ongoing part of the services and plan to gather your data for the final evaluation as part of the process of project management. Only in this way can you demonstrate the results of implementation of the proposal.

In the example, evaluation is to be carried out in two phases: process and product. The process evaluation includes information and answers to the following issues:

1. The working agreement was established with the retirement village. (A copy will be attached as a model for other projects.) Completion date will be no later than April 30.
2. The survey was conducted within the time frame and had at least 60 percent participation by residents. Completion date will be no later than May 31.
3. At least 100 additional titles of large-print books, of appropriate size and weight, were identified and ordered no later than June 30 and received no later than September 30.
4. At least 20 periodicals were identified and ordered no later than June 30 and received no later than November 1.
5. Acquired materials were cataloged no later than November 15.
6. Plans for the circulation center were developed and approved no later than September 30.

7. An initial group of part-time staff, selected from among residents of the center, were hired and oriented no later than December 1.
8. An appropriate opening ceremony was planned, to be carried out no later than December 1.

The product evaluation is organized to provide information and answers to the following:

1. How the objectives of the project were met. Variance will be explained and information provided to assess the success of the project.
2. Circulation rate of books and periodicals during the first six months of the project. Also, the number of participants and their satisfaction with the project will be described. Recommendations will be made (as suggested by this information) to improve circulation participation.
3. Descriptive information will explain the staffing and its effectiveness. Analyses of patterns of staffing, staffing problems, and issues will be carried out. Recommendations for improvement will be made.
4. Additions and expansions to the project will be provided, with funding approaches to support them.
5. Funding to sustain the circulation center, after the period supported through the project, will be described. This will assure the funding agency that efforts will be continued if it is determined that the project is successful in terms of items 1, 2, and 3 of this product evaluation.

Address the need for future funding as well. Funding sources are always interested in what it will take to maintain the services after they have supplied start-up funds and where you plan to get future support. The best plans for future support are those that do not require continuing outside funding (i.e., those that become self-supporting).

Prepare a budget. It should be realistic, accurate, and justifiable. Do not underestimate the cost, thinking you will be more likely to get funding if the budget is small. The budget you prepare should match the objectives and should be easily audited. If there is a need for matching, your budget should be presented in two columns (see figure 29). The matching percentage should represent the amount required by the funding source.

In addition to various ways of identifying matches, your fiscal officers will tell you what indirect or overhead cost to state in your budget. A percentage of your request (established by the institution or city), reflects the cost of administering a grant. (Examples are light, heat, space, bookkeeping, and payroll costs.) This percentage is added to your

Figure 29. Budget for Grant Application

Item	Funds Requested	Local Match
Salaries	_____	_____
Fringe benefits	_____	_____
Consultants and contract services, e.g., bookkeeping, auditing, public relations	_____	_____
Space costs	_____	_____
Rental, lease, and purchase of equipment	_____	_____
Consumable supplies	_____	_____
Travel	_____	_____
Telephone	_____	_____
Other (identify)	_____	_____
Indirect costs @ _____ % (as required by support agency)	_____	_____

budget request, and is occasionally negotiable with the grant-making agency. Whether negotiable or not, it will increase the amount of the request; therefore, it will increase the amount of the required match.

After this work is finished, write a one-page abstract, of the who, why, what, when, where, and cost questions.

Prepare the appendixes, which will include letters of support, statistic, and resumes of the principal investigator and staff.

Review the entire proposal with your staff, your board, and your school or town/city administation.

Submit the application and wait for the money to come. If you are not successful the first time around, do not let your work go to waste. Submit the proposal to another source of funding, or make the changes suggested by the first funding source. In either case, you may have to emphasize a different angle or approach to meet the criteria, with the same tenacity you show every year at your budget presentation.

WHERE TO FIND INFORMATION?

While cuts in library budgets are publicized, we also see that other-than-tax-dollar sources of revenue are tapped by libraries. LSCA, NEH, ECIA, and HEA are familiar acronyms for federal granting agencies and legislation. Less often, we see the names Ford, Lilly, and Kellogg—

foundations that have granted money to support library services of one sort or another.

How can you target grant-making agencies that have supported library services in the past? How can you be sure these sources are interested in funding your proposal? This is where the curiosity and tenacity of a dedicated librarian come into play. How better to use your skills than to help yourself and your library?

General Sources

The *Bowker Annual of Library and Book Trade Information* is the obvious source of information about funding that is directly applicable to libraries. Each year there is a summary of the current status of funding through such programs as the Library Services Construction Act; the Education Consolidation and Improvement Act; the Higher Education Act; the National Endowment for the Humanities; and the National Historical Publications and Records Commission.

Do not stop with the *Bowker Annual*. It describes only legislation and federal programs that have historically supported libraries. If you are in a vocational/technical school, you should look for sources that provide money for that specialty, such as Fund for the Improvement of Post-Secondary Education or the Vocational Education Act. Granting agencies, other than those summarized by *Bowker*, meet a wide variety of needs.

The Annual *Register of Grant Support* (published by Marquis) is a standard reference work on nonrepayable financial support: grant programs of government agencies, public and private foundations, corporations, community trusts, unions, educational and professional associations, and special-interest organizations. The *Register's* indexes provide access by subject, organization and program, geographical location, and personnel.

Federal Government

Published annually by the Office of Management and Budget (OMB), the *Catalog of Federal Domestic Assistance* is a government-wide compendium of federal programs and activities that gives both financial and nonfinancial assistance. It identifies types of assistance, eligibility requirements, program uses and restrictions, agency procedures, and guidelines for the application and award process, along with federal program policies and regulations. Information about the support programs is cross-referenced by functional classification, subject, applicants, deadlines for applications, popular names, authorizing legislation, and federal circular requirements.

Two daily federal publications (to which the *Catalog* refers its readers) are the *Commerce Business Daily* and the *Federal Register*. The *CBD* lists U.S.

government procurement invitations, research and development requests, and contract awards. The *Federal Register* provides rules, regulations, and legal notices issued by federal agencies (as well as proposed rules) and notices of meetings and hearings. The *Catalog* will refer you to one of these daily publications for deadline dates, amendments to funding programs, notices of awards, and other current information.

Foundations

Now we turn to foundations. The *Foundation Grants Index*, published by the Foundation Center, indicates the kinds of grants foundations have supported in the past. This reference book will tell you who might be receptive to your idea. It is a detailed summary of grants given by large private or community foundations. The 1992 *Index* summarizes 57,443 grants, totaling over $4.47 billion, representing 57 percent of total grant dollars awarded by all U.S., private, corporate, and community foundations. The grants (at least $5,000) were given to organizations, rather than individuals. Each foundation is listed alphabetically by state and records of the foundations' grants of $10,000 or more are arranged alphabetically by recipient.

The *Foundation Directory*, also published by the Foundation Center, is the standard reference work for information about nongovernmental foundations in the United States. The 1992 edition includes 2,729 foundations, with assets of $134 billion. The large foundations in the *Foundation Grants Index* are included in this reference book, along with many smaller granting sources.

Arranged alphabetically by state, the entries provide the foundation's name, address, and telephone number; names of donors; a brief statement of purpose (including special limitations); financial data such as assets, gifts received, expenditures, total grants, number of grants paid, and highest and lowest grants; names of officers and trustees; and grant application information.

The indexes to the *Directory* provide access by state and city, foundation names, personnel, and fields of interest. Foundations listed in boldface type under a field of interest make grants on a national or regional basis, while the others generally limit their giving to the city or state in which they are located.

The *National Data Book* (also published by the Foundation Center) gives brief financial profiles of active foundations in the United States, many of which are not listed in the *Foundations Directory*. This information is arranged alphabetically by state. For further information about a foundation listed in this resource, you may write to the foundation directly or consult the Internal Revenue Service information returns that are filed annually by all private foundations. The IRS information returns give full listings of grants made by the foundation in the year of record. The index is arranged alphabetically by the name of the foundations.

In addition to the above mentioned volumes, separate directories are published about the foundations in a particular state or region. A bibliography of these resources is in the *National Data Book*.

The Foundation Center offers still more help to the money hunter. A list of nationwide foundation reference collections (for free public use) is available in each publication issued by the Foundation Center. Also, the Center operates libraries in New York City and Washington, D.C., which contain all public records and printed publications relating to private foundations. Field offices, with extensive collections, are in Cleveland and San Francisco. Cooperating collections are available in all fifty states, Mexico, Puerto Rico, and the Virgin Islands.

Corporations

Corporations may be approached to fund ideas that will give them good publicity and may be viewed as beneficial to their employees. Few corporations make grant guidelines available, nor do they publicize philanthropic objectives or procedures for grant applicants to follow. In 1982, corporate contributions were only 1.77 percent of their pretax net income; however, "corporations have donated the largest percentage of their grants to education in the last four years." (Lefferts, 1982).

While money may be obtained from corporations, the probability of "gifts" to the local or university library, such as books, technical materials, or equipment, should not be overlooked. This is especially true if the local corporate managers work closely with a college or department of a local university. These managers often have an opportunity to determine such gifts.

As a librarian, you should be aware of special alignments between departments or colleges and local business and industry. This may give you an opportunity to discuss special needs with professors and deans, which can be presented to local businesses and industries.

Individuals

A nonprofit organization, such as Friends of the Library, and individual citizens should not be overlooked as other sources of revenue. Most public and school libraries cannot sell their inventory for profit, but they can donate such things as duplicate and out-of-date titles to nonprofit organizations. Friends of the Library, in turn, can hold a book sale and return their profits to the library.

If Friends of the Library assures you of a certain level of funding for the year, this should be put into the regular budget as a "source of income."

However (as is often the case), you cannot honestly project this amount. Therefore it can (and should) be planned and handled as if it were an exceptional source of funds. The same holds true for endowments.

Contributions from individuals can also be solicited. It is helpful to have an established program by which a person who has died can be remembered by friends through book purchases. Bookplates can be prepared in his or her name.

STRATEGY

Now that you know the available resources, what strategy should you use? In general, the government funds what has been done before, is likely to continue funding an ongoing and successful program, and is likely to give funding extensions. It is also likely to give "seed grants" for various ideas. Foundations, on the other hand, like to fund new and innovative ideas and like to know that activities, once begun, will need no more support.

When you look for federal assistance, be sure you know who administers the funds. For instance, you will save yourself time by noting that LSCA funds are administered by state and territorial library administrative agencies. By talking directly with a consultant at your state library, you can get all proposal and funding information from someone close to home.

In no case should you hesitate to telephone a grant-making source for information, instructions, feedback, suggestions, and evaluation of your proposal idea.

Recognizing that corporations respond to local needs, you may want to become aware of the interests of their presidents or chief executive officers. An officer who enjoys hunting is more likely to support a collection of books on guns than a collection on antique cars.

After you have discovered the personal interests of the CEO or the chairman of the board (and prepared a grant proposal), you should approach the corporation at its highest level. All philanthropic decisions are made at the top. All the rules about grant-proposal writing pertain, but it is especially important to define how the corporation will create a good public image as a result of its contribution. For this reason, it is often better to ask a corporation to provide money for equipment than for services. It is also important to emphasize benefits that might accrue to employees (including retired employees) of the business.

It is with local contributions in mind that all Foundation Center publications are arranged by state. People who live in New York, Washington, D.C., or Illinois have many granting sources available to them. Those who live in New Mexico, Arkansas, or Mississippi might better turn to the *Source Book,* which lists the large foundations that operate on a regional or national basis; the *National Data Book,* which lists the small foundations; or the *Annual Register of Grant Support,* which lists a variety of granting agencies.

PRACTICE EXPERIENCES

1. Identify a source of funding and request that it send you its agency's proposal requirements.

2. List the major sources of federal money for public libraries and the agencies through which you might gain access to such funds.

3. Using the three major reference resources mentioned in the text, identify possible funding sources for construction purposes, for acquisition, for staff training.

4. List the major sources of federal money for school libraries and the agencies through which you might gain access to them.

5. Contact a local corporation and determine its potential for assisting your library's funding needs.

SELECTED READINGS

Annual Register of Grant Support: 1992. National Register Publishing Co.

Commerce Business Daily. U.S. Department of Commerce. *Federal Register.* Washington, D.C., National Archives and Records Service.

Foundation Directory. 14th ed. New York: The Foundation Center, 1992.

Foundation Grants Index. 20th ed. New York: The Foundation Center, 1992.

Gaby, Patricia V., and Daniel M. Gaby. *Nonprofit Organizational Handbook: A Guide to Fundraising, Grants, Lobbying, Membership Building, Publicity and Public Relations.* Englewood Cliffs, N.J.: Prentice-Hall, 1979.

Hillman, Howard, and Marjorie Chamberlain. *The Art of Winning Corporate Grants.* New York: Vanguard, 1980.

Lefferts, Robert. *Getting A Grant in the Nineteen Eighties: How to Write Successful Grant Proposals,* 2nd ed. Englewood, NJ: Prentice-Hall. 1982.

Lloyd, Terry. "Winning the Budget Battle; How to Get the Money You Need From the People Who Control It." *Sales & Marketing Management.* Vol. 141, il., April '89 p. 32(5) 49F3091.

Margolin, Judith B., ed. *Foundation Center's User-Friendly Guide: Grantseeker's Guide to Resources.* Foundation Center, 1992.

Proposal Writers' Swipe File III: 15 Professionally Written Grant Proposals in Prototypes of Approaches, Styles, and Structures. Washington, D.C.: Taft Corp., 1981.

9
Writing the Budget Presentation

Most of the parent organizations for libraries want to receive budget proposals from each of their subunits. You should expect an opportunity to not only present the proposed amounts for each line item, but to describe how these amounts were arrived at.

WHY IS WRITING SO CRITICAL?

The budget that you submit to your funding agency is basically one of dollars and cents. The budget is in the appropriate format and contains the specific figures that have been requested, and you have made sure that all of the established guidelines for the various categories have been met. As you complete your list of figures, you are aware of the planning that has gone into the process: The evaluation of needs for library activities and services, the identification of goals and objectives, the analysis of cost alternatives, the prioritizing, and the hard decision making when needs are not met by available funds.

Now after all of this work has been reduced to the final few pages of figures, you fear that much of the information you have is not being transmitted to the people who will ultimately make the decisions about your budget. This may be true to a degree, but the submission of your budget proposal does provide the opportunity to share some of the critical information about the library budget with those people. You can and should write some explanations to accompany your budget proposal.

A PROPOSED FORMAT

It is helpful to organize your written materials into presentation format. There are a number of approaches to take, and the one suggested here is only one illustration. Study your own funding organization and how it operates to determine if there are expected formats for this part of your budget submission. If there are, use those rather than the format suggested here.

It is well to recognize that the fiscal decision makers in your parent organziation will receive many budget requests from divergent suborganizations within their administrative unit. The time and energy required of them is extensive and intense. Therefore, your written materials should be brief and to the point.

The first part of the written materials should provide an overview: What you expect the budget to accomplish—using numbers and examples (percentage increases; changes in activities and services; additional acquisition; special points of focus, etc.). This should generally not exceed one page.

Next, identify and explain major shifts in emphasis (if any) in your pattern of activities and services. These changes can be either expansions or reductions. Explain the reason(s) for each one briefly (a sentence or two should suffice). If there have been changes in the numbers of personnel in various categories, be specific in presenting your strategies for these.

Finally, if there have been any additional issues that have been involved in your budget decision making that need to be addressed, briefly explain the impact of each on the budget.

STRATEGY

You cannot consistently ask for more than you can get. If you do, you will lose credibility with the funding agency. You must "read the signs" of political realities. Often, a city or school administration will request that the budget reflect no more than a 2 to 10 percent increase. Today, more likely, the trend is to *reduce* the budget by 2 to 10 percent.

On the other hand, do not shortchange your budget. Realize that there are definite roles that people in the funding process are expected to play. When someone steps outside his or her role, the whole process is jeopardized. There are boards of trustees that, instead of advocating a library's budget, cut it. Then the budget, already trimmed of all fat, is presented to the funding agency, which, as a matter of course, cuts it again.

It is easier for a board or funding agency to cut items that are listed separately. For example, if you lump all library supplies together with the book budget in a Materials and Supplies line item, you will be less likely to run out of money to buy charge cards and overdue notices. If you itemize supplies, the funding agency may be tempted to take issue with some of your specific needs.

If you know the budget will be cut, it may be better to lump items together so that the cut will be across the board and decisions about how to spend the remaining money are yours. Once the funding agency tells you to cut the money in your Equipment line, which would have been spent on a new microfilm cabinet, but leaves you the money to buy a microfilm reader, you cannot buy the cabinet instead, because the reader is of no use to you without storage for the film. It is wise to establish priorities on the equipment you need. If you share that information with the funding agency, it is more likely to cut items you feel are less vital, instead of using its amateur judgment. Remember:

> You can have two or three items which are priority 1.
> You have to justify the need for all new equipment.

Don't assume that, because you have set priorities on equipment items, the board will agree with you.

Be aware of the difficulty that may arise if you want to eliminate a service in order to decrease your budget. Branch libraries occasionally are not cost effective, but political realities may be such that stopping their operation would anger enough citizens to influence next year's appropriation negatively. There may be services you have to maintain, against your better judgment, because your clientele (or a member of your funding agency) wants them.

Be aware, also, of the activities and services your community supports. The school board in an Eastern town cut a teacher position to meet the budgetary constraints required by the town's finance committee. During a town meeting, the residents voted to reinstate that money in the budget. Thus a shrewd administrator can use community support to get full funding, even while he or she plays the game required by the officials.

BASICS OF THE WRITTEN BUDGET PRESENTATION

Line-Item Budget

The line-item format presents a three-year history to the funding agency, citing the

> amount appropriated and spent the previous year,

amount requested, appropriated, and spent during the current
year, and the
amount requested for the next year.

Since the items on each line of the budget are not tied in to any
activities or services, neither their rationale nor their effectiveness is
questioned. The budget presentation need explain only the percentage
increase/decrease of each item, and special attention need be paid only
to items that increase more than the expected percent. Special attention
should also be given to explaining any decrease in an item. You don't
have to treat increases or decreases equally. Focus on the issues that are
politically salable.

Line-Item Presentation

Using the line-item budget sheets in figure 30, we will hypothesize the
fiscal year 1994 request. The guidelines allow for a 5 percent across-the-
board salary increase, a 2 percent increase in supplies, and an 8 percent
increase in light and heat. The budget is not to exceed a 2 percent
increase.

Noticeable changes in the line items result from the proposed
purchase of an IBM personal computer for the use of patrons. As a
result of this one-time capital outlay, you plan to maintain the acquisition budget as is, although $2,500 will be shifted from print to nonprint
to allow you to purchase at least five software packages. The training
budget increases 43 percent to bring the staff up to date. All other
increases conform with the guidelines; so your presentation might look
like the following outline.

I. With a 7 percent increase, the library will:
    A. Provide a 5 percent across-the-board increase to staff.
    B. Purchase a computer for use by patrons.
    C. Purchase a minimum of 5 software programs for use by
       patrons.
    D. Train the library staff to use and teach the use of the computer.
    E. Maintain the acquisition budget at its present level.
II. Access to a computer will:
    A. Answer the requests received from 70 percent of adult pa-
       trons through a survey conducted in January.
    B. Reinforce its everyday usefulness to the parents of students
       who are learning to use computers in school.
    C. Allow students who do not have home computers to have
       computer access.
III. The provided software programs will:

       A. Offer the services requested by adults who answered the survey: word processing, computer language learning, and budgeting.

IV. Training the library staff will:

       A. Prepare staff for the new technology.

       B. Allow staff to teach prospective users to use the computer.

       C. Assure that a trained person is available at all times.

V. Maintaining the acquisition budget at its current level will:

       A. Decrease the number of titles purchased and processed by 15 percent.

       B. Increase the time technical services staff can spend learning and training patrons to use the computer.

       C. Be consistent with the library's statistics that show a decline in circulation of print materials.

The Budget

The function budget format provides the opportunity for you to describe the various activities and services, with their key goals and objectives. Typically, you can present the most cost effective/efficient strategies for achieving those outcomes and build a powerful case for acceptance of your requests.

Alternatives for fulfilling the goals and objectives do not need to be exhaustive, and a shrewd presenter would use them only to contrast the more positive results to be obtained by the recommended strategies and requested funding levels.

One of the most effective methods is to highlight changes in existing and new services in the main text. Established services that are not changing (except through approved incremental increases or decreases) can be assumed to be approved and therefore noncontroversial.

Presenting services priorities and the funds needed to support each is a final step in preparing the written presentation for function budgeting. This can be a tabular chart, which can easily be scanned by the reader, but it must accurately summarize the recommended activities and services and levels of funding for each (see figure 31).

Activity Presentation

If we use the same data in the line-item budget, the computer literacy and acquisitions activity could be presented as follows:

    Computer literacy has become as important as learning to read. The need has been identified through a survey distributed to adult library users in January. To meet this need, the library will:

Figure 30. Line-Item Budget for Submission (in dollars)

Account Number	Account Title	Actual Expenditures, FY '91	Actual Expenditures, FY '92	Appropriation, FY '93	Actual Expenditures, though Dec. '93	Estimated Expenditures, FY '94	Requested for FY '94
100	Personnel services	259,447	267,231	280,592	140,296	280,592	294,622
300	Materials & supplies	70,611	72,729	76,366	38,396	74,324	76,795
400	Contractual services	45,669	47,034	49,386	25,511	49,386	59,554
500	Lease/purchase	2,000	2,060	2,075	1,038	2,075	2,137
600	Capital outlay	1,826	1,882	2,063	—	0	6,294
Total		379,553	390,936	410,482	205,241	406,377	439,402
100	Personnel services	259,447	267,231	280,592	140,296	280,592	294,622
310	Print materials	60,908	62,736	65,875	31,046	63,883	63,375
320	Nonprint	1,770	1,870	1,914	1,800	1,914	4,414
330	Office	3,272	3,375	3,538	1,500	3,488	3,715
335	Custodial	1,947	2,000	2,160	2,000	2,160	2,268
340	Electrical	1,770	1,775	1,914	1,200	1,914	2,010
345	Plumbing	708	730	765	650	765	803
350	Safety	236	243	200	200	200	210
Total		70,611	72,729	76,366	38,396	74,324	76,795

405	Postage	1,104	1,137	1,472	1,472	1,472	1,693
410	Telephone	1,922	1,998	2,078	1,039	2,078	2,390
415	Light & heat	25,464	26,209	28,239	14,120	28,239	35,299
420	Water	295	303	319	160	319	351
430	Printing	1,123	1,100	1,012	400	1,012	1,063
435	Microfilm	1,121	1,208	1,212	1,000	1,212	1,273
440	Binding	826	853	891	290	891	936
445	Auto. maint.	110	110	120	60	120	132
450	Leased equip.	564	588	612	306	612	673
455	Bldg. maint.	12,685	13,060	13,018	6,509	13,018	14,320
460	Training	354	364	304	100	304	1,304
470	Service contracts	101	104	109	55	109	120
	Total	45,669	47,034	49,386	25,511	49,386	59,554
510	Computer	—	—	—	—	—	—
520	Copy machine	1,200	1,236	1,296	648	1,296	1,335
530	Stationwagon	800	824	779	390	779	802
	Total	2,000	2,060	2,075	1,038	2,075	2,137
610	Furniture	—	800	114	0	0	0
615	Equipment	1,249	441	1,294	0	0	6,294
620	AV equip.	577	641	655	0	0	0
	Total	1,826	1,882	2,063	0	0	6,294

Figure 31. Function Budget for Submission

	Computer Literacy	Acquisitions	Total
Personnel Services	$36,816	$29,453	$ 66,269
Materials & supplies	2,500	65,289	67,789
Contractual services	1,500	—	1,500
Capital outlay	5,000	—	5,000
Total	$45,816	$94,742	$140,558

1. Purchase a personal computer for patrons to use in the library by September 1994.
2. Purchase software packages requested by adults who answered a survey: word processing, spread sheet, and language training by September 1994.
3. Train all 30 library staff members to use the computer by October 1994.
4. Schedule biweekly use classes for groups of no more than 6 adults no later than November 1994, to be taught by reference and technical service librarians.
5. Schedule 4 hours every afternoon for students, no later than October 1994.

By maintaining the acquisition budget at the same level, we will:

1. Purchase 15 percent fewer print titles during fiscal year 1994.
2. Purchase software packages by September 1994.
3. Decrease staff needed to process print titles by 12.5 FTE.
4. Free 12.5 FTE staff to train themselves and others to use the computer by October 1994.

STAFF INPUT

Once the presentation is written, share it with members of your staff. Since they probably know more about the library than members of the funding agency, and are "tuned into" some of the misconceptions held by the public, they can critique your presentation in a helpful way.

Ask your staff to identify words that are used by librarians but often are meaningless to the public. You may be too close to library jargon to recognize them. Examples are:

jobber	machine-readable data	serials
periodicals	YA programming	OCLC
cataloging	com catalog	retrospective conversion
classification	shelflist	reconciliation of serials holdings
serials checklist	bibliographic tools	searching

By opening yourself to the questions of your staff, you will be able to plug holes and delete and add information that will make your presentation more persuasive.

Both the accomplishments and limitations of the library should be addressed in the written proposal. This may be the only time of the year that these stakeholders, the funding agency and your staff, recognize the strides made by the organization and the part they play. A morale builder for your staff, the presentation may solicit ongoing interest from members of the funding board or agency.

Since you will have the opportunity to supplement your written presentation with a verbal one, write briefly and clearly. You will be able to expand on the documentation during your in-person presentation.

PRACTICE EXPERIENCES

1. Using your library's budget format, write a presentation for two line items or two activities or services.

2. Pretend you are a member of the funding board, and attack the two budget presentations in this chapter. What questions would you ask the library director during the verbal presentation?

3. Maintaining the acquistions budget at its present level is fairly unusual. What risks might this approach run? What benefit might accrue?

4. Prepare a defense for the maintenance of the acquisition budget at the same level in the face of a 5 percent recision demand for the budget as a whole.

SELECTED READINGS

Burkhead, Jesse, and Paul Bringewatt. *Municipal Budgetline: A Primer for Elected Officials.* Washington,D.C.: Joint Center for Political Studies, 1974.

Gasteiger, Daniel. "Spreadsheet Reports Primer." *PC-Computing*, Vol. 5, October '92 p. 302(1).

Lefferts, Robert. *How to Prepare Charts and Graphs for Effective Reports.* New York: Harper, 1982.

Robb, Margaret Y., and Richard Scoville. "Tips for Great Reports." *PC World*, Vol. 10, April '92 p. 224(7).

Zinsser, William. *On Writing Well.* Third Edition. New York: Harper & Row. 1985.

10
In-Person Presentations

In-person presentations by organizational subunits are often required to provide the formal decision makers with face-to-face information about budget proposals. These presentations are often called "budget hearings" or "budget reviews." Usually, you might expect to have two levels of such hearings: one with your own board and one with a review unit of your parent organization.

Such encounters provide an excellent opportunity for you to make a good case for your library budget. There are many fears and frustrations for all managers as a result of these reviews, but there are methods that can reduce the fear and frustration and help you to be an effective spokesperson for the library.

This chapter will suggest ideas and approaches you might take to gain approval of the library budget.

Presenting your budget proposal to a decision-making board allows you to benefit from personal contact and two-way communication. This is your opportunity to

Ensure that the board understands your operation and your funding needs.
Provide details and address the doubts of board members.
Influence the decision makers.

ANTICIPATING THE IN-PERSON ORAL PERSENTATION

You need to gather important background information before your presentation:

When will you be heard?
Where will you be heard?

117

What will your time constraints be?
Who will be your audience?
What are the board's expectations regarding the presentation?
Are there rules or traditions about which you should know?
What will happen before and after your presentation?

Most of the time, answers to these questions are not volunteered by those who arrange the meetings. You may want to attend presentations made by other department heads or organizational subunits or you may rely on your contacts to give you the "inside information" you need.

TIMING IS EVERYTHING

You may not be given the choice of hearing time or place, but it will not hurt to request what is best for you. If there is a comfortable meeting room in the library, invite the board to your territory. In this way you gain some control of the timing and the comfort of your audience.

By bringing the board to the library, you can give the members a tour of the facilities, thereby bringing your programs and needs to light in a special way. In addition, you can arrange the meeting room to your liking, eliminating intimidating aspects, and you can ensure everyone's comfort.

Advertising executives, trying to sell their campaigns to prospective clients, try to make their presentation either first or last, either of which ensures a memorable presentation. Of course, if you are not well prepared, you *won't want* to be remembered.

If you are allotted 9:45 to 10:00 p.m. on a week night, you would prepare a different presentation than if you were given a 9:45 to 10:00 a.m. hearing. The hearings may begin at 7 p.m., and as the evening wears on and the preceding hearings exceed their scheduled time slots, *your* hearing may be delayed until close to midnight. By that time, of course, you will confront a tired and irritated audience. Thus a concise, interesting, and entertaining presentation will be a necessity.

Since this is your chance to explain and persuade, you must assess your audience. Find out who they are.

Are they or their families library users?
Do they have children in school, or in the preschool story hour?
What areas of town do they live in?
In which school or branch library will they have a personal interest?
To which interests of theirs can you appeal?

Also, assess how much they know about the library, their beliefs and values, their attitudes toward you and the library program. During your presentation you will appeal to both the intellect and the emotions of the funding board. Try to persuade them of your need by appealing to their logic, but appeal also to their

> Pride ("If we launch this program, we will be one of twenty libraries in the forefront of a trend that will sweep the nation.")
>
> Competitiveness ("You'll be shocked to learn that ours is the only library in the state without a telephone.")
>
> Indignation ("Are we going to sit here and do nothing while our competitor lures our patrons away?")

These examples further emphasize the need to know the value and belief systems of your audience.

If you are addressing a group of nonreaders, who see budgets as no more than ploys to take money from their pockets, you should have a more formal and persuasive presentation than if the group values education and sees budgeting as a tool for better management of a motherhood-and-apple-pie institution. Obviously, these are two extremes, but probably both extremes will be represented on your decision-making board or in your parent organization.

You need to determine, both formally and informally, what rules and traditions are observed within the organization during presentations. Usually you can find out about formal rules by asking your immediate superior. However, it is well to remember that, in addition to formal rules, traditions or customs have often developed within the organization as a part of these public processes. Some of them relate to how to address various persons, where to sit or stand, or if it is permissable to have staff members present to help answer questions, or to participate in the presentation.

There are two ways to obtain such information, both of which should be used. Inquire of one of your inside, informal sources and attend presentations by other units of the parent organization. Use the information and observations to help you with *your* presentation plans.

It is also helpful to know what usually happens before and after your presentation. How much material do you need to provide the hearing group in advance? Are there informal discussions that should or must be carried out? With whom and when? Are you expected to initiate follow-up discussions and provide additional information? The people to answer such questions are the same as those cited above: your immediate superior and your informal contacts.

ORGANIZING YOUR PRESENTATION

Since your purpose is to inform and persuade, you need to master the deductive, inductive, and eliminative methods of organizing your presentation.

Deductive reasoning moves forward from a statement or premise that must be accepted as true by everyone you are talking with. This premise is used together with facts or other premises to develop particular arguments or plans of action.

Be careful in choosing a premise on which to base your presentation. Librarians often feel that the importance of education, reading, and libraries is self-evident. They may begin budget presentations by stating that "libraries are basic to one's happiness." Unfortunately, this premise does not have unanimous support. Indeed, library support may be in inverse relation to budgetary demands of life-sustaining institutions (i.e., police and fire departments).

Since deductive reasoning moves from generalization to specifics, the line-item, incremental budget is a good candidate for deductive presentation. Whether the budgetary guidelines limit you to a 10 percent increase or require a 3 percent decrease is a premise on which you should build your presentation. If you act on this premise, your argument will be persuasive. The line-item budget is easy to defend, as long as you stay within the guidelines, because tradition expects percentage adjustments.

As a school librarian, you might begin your deductive reasoning by stating: "The school library exists to support and supplement the school curriculum." It is hard to believe that anyone would disagree with that statement, but you may have to prove it before you gain consensus and can continue with your presentation. Once you are convinced that everyone agrees with that premise, you might explain that the curriculum expanded during the year to include creative writing, two foreign languages, and office management. "Therefore, we need $4,000 to buy materials to support these new curricula."

Inductive reasoning moves from specifics to create a generalization. Usually, this means building on a series of facts that result in a conclusion. Fact: "Circulation has increased 100 percent during this fiscal or school year." Fact: "Staff has decreased by 0.5 FTE during this fiscal or school year." Fact: "There is a two-week lag between the return of books to the library and their return to the shelves." Fact: "Accessibility of materials to users has decreased proportionately." Conclusion: "Pages must be hired to reshelve materials. This is the reason for a $700 increase in the circulation program."

Function budget formats are well suited to inductive presentations. By using function budgeting, you begin with a number of activities and services that create the entirety of the operations of the library. By gaining support for each component, you establish that these activities and services are worth supporting. From those specifics, you can accumulate support for the whole.

You can picture the shape of this argument as a pyramid: you make a series of statements which, together, provide the base for the apex or conclusion.

Eliminative reasoning allows you to identify a problem, then address the alternative solutions, eliminating each until only one remains. You can fall into traps with this method if you have not considered *all* the alternatives and if their rejection is not clearly conceived. Alternative solutions usually have advantages *and* disadvantages. Sometimes one clearly outweighs the other, but all too often they depend on opinion, and the opinions of board members may differ from yours.

VISUAL PRESENTATION

The most common presentation is a lecture. But because audiences retain only about 20 percent of what they hear, and 50 percent of what they see and hear, you will want to prepare visual aids: slides or a slide/tape presentation, charts and graphs on chalkboard or flip chart, overhead transparencies, and/or a videotape. The room arrangement, equipment availability, and preparation time will determine which method(s) you use.

A slide/tape presentation requires the ability to darken and arrange the room for ease of viewing, requires equipment, and is time consuming in preparation. It is, on the other hand, an effective way of bringing the library to life.

Charts and graphs require a wall or easel, and require less time to prepare. Moreover, you can focus your audience on the specifics you wish to highlight. If you use charts or graphs, be sure there is plenty of "white space." If you present a table, present no more than three or four columns per visual, and do not talk more than about one minute with any one visual.

Overhead transparencies require an overhead projector and screen, and no more time to prepare than charts and graphs. Your presentation can be drawn, printed, or typed onto a piece of paper that can be made into a transparency by a photocopier. When you present word visuals, highlight what you say by using key words. Never use complete sentences. Use no more than seven words per line and limit the visual to eight lines. By following these rules of thumb you will ensure the necessary "white space."

As videotapes have become common, they are used more and more often during budget presentations. They require a somewhat darkened room, a particular seating arrangement, and special equipment, and can be time consuming to prepare. But this medium brings the library to life by providing action.

Remember, any visuals used, including videotapes, are a supplement to your oral presentation, not a substitute for it. You are still presenting the library budget.

ARE THERE ANY QUESTIONS?

You needn't flinch when you hear the moderator of the hearing board ask for questions. It's an opportunity, if you have done your homework.

"Yes, I have a question," says Mr. Brown. "I still don't see what will be gained from a deposit library at the rest home in the Heights."

Having done your homework, you know that Mr. Brown's mother-in-law lives in a different rest home, and you might respond this way:

"Our survey of library users showed a lower representation from that home than others. We plan to pilot a deposit library in that home. If it's successful, we may be able to accommodate other homes in town."

"How many of your program participants are residents of this city?" asks Mr. Smith."

"I'm happy to report that the proportion of residents to out-of-towners has doubled since last year, Mr. Smith."

Knowing that Mr. Smith does not want to support anyone outside his tax base, you have prepared for this question. (Be sure not to say *too* much.)

"What I want clarified," insists Mr. Jones, "is the meaning behind that flap I read about last month."

Don't assume you know what "that flap" refers to. Don't answer too quickly.

"What flap, Mr. Jones? Was it something you read in a magazine?"

"No, no, no. I saw something about a library conference in the newspaper. It was held in Chicago. Why weren't you there?"

What started as a challenge can suddenly be turned to your advantage.

"Yes, that *was* an excellent opportunity. I didn't attend because we didn't have sufficient travel funds. I've recommended a travel budget this year of $600. Luckily, the conference will be nearer home and I'll be able to attend and report back to you."

By restating the question and having it clarified, you gain better understanding of the motive behind the question, as well as time to formulate a response.

"How exactly do the circulation figures compare between the high school and the junior high school?" demands Ms. Gray, the newest member of the funding board—a question you hadn't anticipated. Moreover, the statistics are not readily available. What do you say?

"I don't have those statistics handy, Ms. Gray. I'll pull them together and get them to you tomorrow."

It is better to be straight forward (no apologies are necessary) than to respond uncertainly. A guess may mar credibility or raise more questions.

Why is Ms. Gray interested in those statistics? You might probe by asking:

"Are you interested in any other data?"

"No. I'm thinking that one way to cut our costs would be to shorten the hours of whichever library is used least."

This gives you information. Now you know her motive, and you can give her information regarding the in-library use of material, the use of facilities, and the use of the reference staff, as well as the circulation figures. Your new board member needs to be oriented and educated about library uses and needs.

Besides identifying board members who need education, the question-and-answer period offers you a chance to witness an exchange of views among board members. You can learn a great deal about the individuals' values and assumptions through their group interaction. Every detail will make next year's presentation easier.

THE CRITIQUE

You have made the best presentation that you knew how to make. There is always room for improvement. Whether it is the procedure of the board to act on requests immediately or take them under advisement until *their* entire budget is completed, you have had your input.

Therefore, as soon as possible after the end of the presentation, make notes to yourself:

> What unanswered questions and requests for information do you need to provide? To whom? By when?
> What do you feel were the strongest and the weakest parts of the presentation? Why? What changes could you have made?
> What issues arose that you hadn't anticipated?
> Would alternative media have been more helpful at any point?

Make sure you follow up with preferred or requested information promptly. Then relax and wait for further budget negotiations with representatives of your parent organization and/or final approval of your library budget.

PRACTICE EXPERIENCES

1. List at least five important background-information items you should identify before you plan your in-person presentation.

2. Explain briefly why these are important for the presenter to understand.

3. Discuss the significance of formal and informal rules to the presenter.

4. Differentiate between inductive and deductive reasoning and explain how each might be used in a presentation.

5. Choose a visual presentation and, using that method, prepare a portion of a presentation.

6. Discuss the in-person practices currently in use with the contact person in your parent organization. If you are a student, discuss this subject with a working librarian.

7. Assuming a 5 percent overall recision, what will be your major emphasis during your in-person presentation?

8. Using 7 above as your foundation, what questions and answers will you anticipate for which you can prepare?

9. Summarize the questions that must be answered while one prepares a budget presentation.

10. Summarize uses to which you can put a question-and-answer period.

SELECTED READINGS

Boettinger, Henry M. *Moving Mountains: Or the Art and Craft of Letting Others See Things Your Way.* New York: Macmillan, 1975.

Gronbeck, Bruce E. *The Articulate Person.* 2nd ed. Glenview, Ill.: Scott, Foresman, 1983.

Guth, Chester K., and Stanley S. Shaw. *How to Put on Dynamic Meetings: Teaming the Oral with the Visual.* Reston, Va.: Reston, 1980.

11
Managing the Budget

MANAGING THE MANAGEMENT TOOL

Once prepared and approved, your budget will become a management tool that will minimize expenditure decisions during the year. Although it helps you manage your library, *you* have to manage it, you have to expend your appropriation in a controlled, legal, and accountable way.

It is politically wise to spend all appropriated money. To underspend suggests miscalculations in your projections and implies that your requested budget was high, so that future budget requests may be disregarded. To overspend is not only bad management, but illegal. You have a legal obligation to spend appropriated money the way you said you would during budget hearings. This means that if your funding board has approved a capital outlay expenditure for carpeting, you should not change your mind and use that money to purchase drapes. Similarly, you usually cannot move money from one account to another without permission from the funding board. This chapter will deal in depth with the purchasing of materials and supplies and the management of petty cash; other items are more routine and will not require as much of your time and energies. For instance, your payroll responsibilities will be discharged by verifying time worked by each employee through a timesheet. You need at least a daily accounting sheet for logging the working hours of each employee (something like figure 32) and/or a system that you manage on your PC. The personnel codes of the parent organization indicate payment or nonpayment of salary for absences as they occur. You can complete such timesheets accurately and simply.

Without a timekeeping system, it is almost impossible to be certain of what has happened in the period covered by the payroll. Do not trust yourself to remember these kinds of details, even if you have only a small

Figure 32. Daily Staff Absence Report

Page _____ of _____

Person Absent			Hours Absent	Substitute		Periods	Comments
Last Name	First Name	Code		Last Name	First Name		

Absence Codes

21	Employee Illness	34	Paid Absence, Other
31	Professional	41	Annual
32	Legal Summons	51	Leave without Pay
33	Bereavement	54	Personal

staff for whom you are responsible. Memory is not sufficient, and examination of your records will be part of almost any audit. Figure 33 is a completed timesheet for an employee for a two-week period. While the interval may vary from one week to one month, biweekly is typical. Explanations on the sheet explain the various entries. Your organization may have other requirements, so you should have your payroll office explain them to you so that you are comfortable with the system in use.

If you have a PC available for use, you may wish to create or copy a timekeeping system for your employees. Check with managers of other units within your parent organization and see if such a system is already in use. If it is, you may be able to borrow the program and install it in your PC without any violation of copyright. Another possibility is to create your own using a spread sheet or Windows on your PC. If you do not feel comfortable with this procedure, call a local university or community college and see if you can provide an "internship" for a student studying data processing or accounting with the agreement that they would create this and other systems for use on your PC.

Paying rent, paying leases, and such routine contractual obligations that fall within your budget are usually taken care of through your parent organization's accounting office. Therefore, once you have approved these obligations and sent the approval documents to accounting, you may not be involved in the actual payments. If you are, usually you will be asked to prepare a purchase requisition to cover each billing or payment period. This process (discussed later in this chapter) is identical for all such actions, except for the cost account code and the description of the authorization.

Utilities are usually handled through the accounting office as well. If they are not, the purchase requisition process is followed, using the appropriate fund account.

FUND ACCOUNTS

Most budgets are divided into classes or groups of fund accounts, such as Personnel, Operating Expenses, Employee Benefits, Purchased Services, Lease-Purchase Equipment, Capital Outlay, and Materials (see Chapter 3). Usually, a fund account number is assigned by the central accounting department for each line item on the budget. For example, the Personnel account number might be 100 and each breakdown within (librarians, aides, clerical, custodial) might be 110, 120, 130, and 140 respectively. Operating Expenses might be 200; Benefits, 300; Purchased Services, 400; Lease-Purchase Equipment, 500; Capital Outlay, 600; and Materials, 700.

Figure 33. Pay Period Time Record (Biweekly)

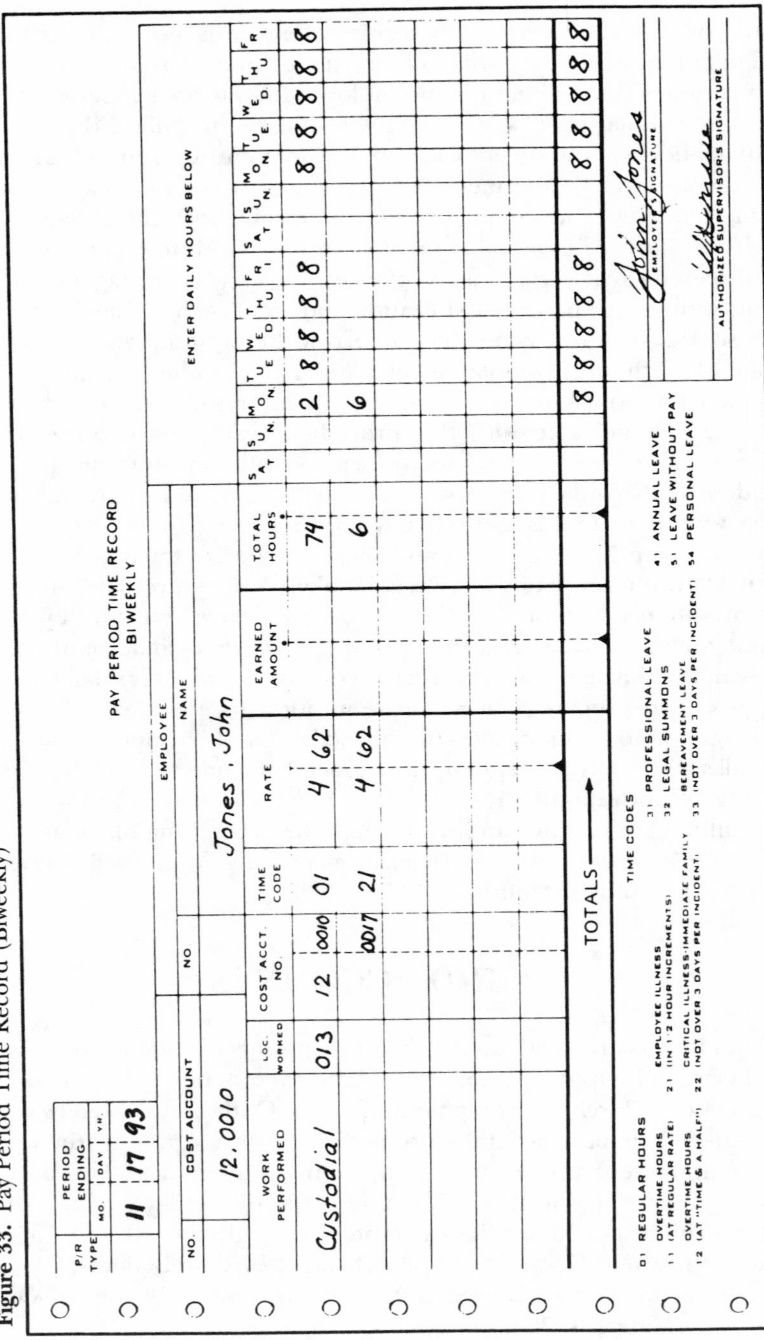

PAY PERIOD TIME RECORD
BIWEEKLY

P/R TYPE	PERIOD ENDING MO.	DAY	YR.
	11	17	93

NO.	COST ACCOUNT	EMPLOYEE NO.	EMPLOYEE NAME
	12.0010		Jones, John

ENTER DAILY HOURS BELOW

WORK PERFORMED	LOC. WORKED	COST ACCT. NO.	TIME CODE	RATE	EARNED AMOUNT	TOTAL HOURS	SAT	SUN	MON	TUE	WED	THU	FRI	SAT	SUN	MON	TUE	WED	THU	FRI
Custodial	013	12 0010	01	4 62		74			2	8	8	8	8			8	8	8	8	8
		0017	21	4 62		6			6											
TOTALS →									8	8	8	8	8			8	8	8	8	8

TIME CODES

01 REGULAR HOURS
11 OVERTIME HOURS (AT REGULAR RATE)
12 OVERTIME HOURS (AT "TIME & A HALF")
21 EMPLOYEE ILLNESS (IN 1/2 HOUR INCREMENTS)
22 CRITICAL ILLNESS-IMMEDIATE FAMILY (NOT OVER 3 DAYS PER INCIDENT)
31 PROFESSIONAL LEAVE
32 LEGAL SUMMONS
33 BEREAVEMENT LEAVE (NOT OVER 3 DAYS PER INCIDENT)
41 ANNUAL LEAVE
51 LEAVE WITHOUT PAY
54 PERSONAL LEAVE

John Jones
EMPLOYEE'S SIGNATURE

AUTHORIZED SUPERVISOR'S SIGNATURE

In many localities you may be allowed to spend money originally intended for clerical support (130) on aides (120) because you are using funds intended for personnel for that purpose. You may not be allowed to move money from the 700s, which support materials, into operating expenses (200). In other words, you may not use money intended to buy books to pay your skyrocketing heating bills.

There are situations in which such restrictions are more or less stringent. Talk with your institution's accountant to learn the rules that govern you. Your flexibility will depend on the answers you get.

PURCHASING MATERIALS

Although you purchase materials and services throughout the year, you begin by making a request to expend, otherwise known as a *purchase requisition (PR)*. If you are the control agent, you have to verify the propriety of the purchase and the availability of funds. Usually, the PR is forwarded to the accounting department for recording in the fund account. This provides a double check on the availability of funds and it provides input into the reports you receive from the accounting department. An order is then placed with the vendor or supplier, usually by the purchasing department, in the form of a *purchase order (PO)*. With increasing frequency, these two forms are combined into a *requisition purchase order (RPO)*.

When the goods are delivered or the services rendered, someone must verify the delivery or completion of the service by initialing or signing the invoice. This certifies that payment can be made. In other words, this "vouches" for the delivery of goods or services. The purchase order and invoice are then gathered together to form a document that testifies to and records the entire transaction. The document, usually called a *voucher*, is forwarded to the central accounting office, where the check is written, and mailed to the vendor.

PURCHASE RECORDS

If you receive monthly accounting reports, you may not have to keep records of expenditures. If reports are less frequent or unavailable, you will need to set up a *ledger*. A three-ring binder, which allows easy insertion or deletion of pages, is ideal. It should be arranged by account numbers, with one page per account, and it might look like figure 34. (This example is for account number 710, from which books are purchased. At the

Figure 34. Ledger Entries

Date of Entry 1992	Name of Vendor	Date of Invoice	Invoice No.	Amount	Balance
July 1					$50,000
August 4	Josten's	7/05/93	076	$ 500	49,500
4	Doubleday	7/15/93	113	250	
5	Prentice-Hall	7/15/93	115	1,400	47,850

beginning of the fiscal year, it had a balance of $50,000, which reflects the budgeted amount.)

Again, if you have a PC available, you may want to obtain or create a system for automating your internal purchasing records (see Chapter 12). While this may seem somewhat time consuming at the beginning, you will find it simpler and easier to utilize. Such records, whether kept by hand or on your PC, are used to keep you "on top" of your budget during the year. You do not have to wait for the periodic reports from your accounting office to know where you are, and when they do come you have your records for a cross-check. You frequently will be more accurate than the accounting office since you have immediate contact with suppliers and therefore know about changes as they occur.

INTERNAL RECORDS

Even if you receive frequent accounting reports, you will want to keep internal records to help you make decisions about spending. Two such reports are *book encumbrances* and *released funds* caused by turnover of personnel.

Buying books, serials, and audiovisual materials presents problems not found with other purchases. When an order is placed you do not know what discount (if any) you will receive; sometimes you do not know the list price of the item, or the shipping charge; and you cannot be sure that every title you order will be forthcoming (the book may have been advertised but not yet published; the publisher or jobber may be out of stock; or the item may be out of print). Since most governmental accounting systems do not carry unexpended funds into the next fiscal year, you have to keep track of ordered, received, and paid-for purchases during the current fiscal year. This presents serious problems near the end of each fiscal year, when you try to spend a specific amount of money on materials whose arrival you cannot predict. To lessen the problem, you can

Overencumber your appropriated amount by a specified time near the end of the fiscal year, such as April 1.

Ask your jobber to send you updated invoices for materials received in the month of June.

With help from your vendor, you can date an invoice to suit your budgetary needs: either pay for it in the current fiscal year or, if you are overexpended, date the invoice "July" and pay for it out of next year's appropriations.

ENCUMBRANCES

To carry this off, you have to accurately and carefully keep track of your encumbrances. Remember, encumbrances are formal commitments for spending the money in your budget. For instance, when you sign a purchase order but have not received the item, the money you have committed to that purchase is *encumbered*. If your parent organization is on a cash accounting system your encumbrances must be cleared before the end of the budget year. That is, ordered items must be received and paid for before the year is over. Normally, items encumbered but not received must be canceled, rather than carried over into the next year. However, if your parent organization is on an accrual accounting system, encumbrances may be carried over to the next year.

This type of internal tracking of your expenditures and encumbrances is also vital to you if your parent organization moves into a recision budgeting mode during the fiscal year. Having accurate and up-to-date information at your finger tips assists you in making those hard decisions that are often necessary in today's budgetary world.

Receiving news of a recision of 3–5 percent is hard enough to deal with, but trying to deal with it when you are largely in the dark about the condition of your budget lines can put you in an almost impossible management position.

Your fiscal account records are nearly always kept in the accounting department of the parent organization, since that is where transactions are carried out (final authorizations for checks to be written). However, to be aware of the status of your accounts, you may want to prepare a ledger sheet like figure 35. This ledger may be one that you handle manually, or one created on your PC. "Date" refers to date of entry into the ledger. "Doc." (document) and "Doc. #" (document number) identify the authorization form for ordering. When the document is a voucher, it refers back to the purchase order; and when the document is a purchase order, it refers back to the purchase requisition.

Figure 35. Ledger Sheet with Encumbrances

Date	Doc.	Doc. #	Vou. #	PO#	Expd.	Expd. Year to Date	Encum.	Encum. Year to Date	Present Balance
									$1,000.00
7/1	PO	1		1			$ 100.00	$100.00	900.00
7/1	PO	2		2			50.00	150.00	850.00
7/1	PO	3		3			30.00	180.00	820.00
7/1	PO	4		4			200.00	380.00	620.00
7/6	Vou	101	101	1	$ 50.00	$ 50.00	(50.00)	330.00	620.00
7/6	Vou	102	102	2	50.00	100.00	(50.00)	280.00	620.00
7/6	Vou	103	103	4	190.00	290.00	(200.00)	80.00	630.00
7/7	PO	5		5			30.00	110.00	600.00
7/8	PO	6		6			100.00	210.00	500.00
7/9	Vou	103.5	103.5	1	40.00	330.00	50.00	160.00	510.00
7/9	PO	7		7			60.00	220.00	450.00
7/9	Vou	104	104	6	110.00	440.00	(100.00)	120.00	440.00
7/10	Vou	105	105	3	30.00	470.00	(30.00)	90.00	440.00
8/1	PO	8		8			300.00	390.00	140.00
8/1	PO	9		9			20.00	410.00	120.00
8/19	Vou	106	106	8	200.00	670.00	(200.00)	210.00	120.00
8/21	Vou	107	107	7	50.00	720.00	(60.00)	150.00	130.00
8/29	Vou	108	108	8	120.00	840.00	(100.00)	50.00	110.00
9/4	PO	10		10			60.00	110.00	50.00
9/6	PO	11		11			50.00	160.00	-0-
9/15	Vou	109	109	5	35.00	875.00	(30.00)	130.00	(5.00)
9/31	Vou	110	110	10	40.00	915.00	(60.00)	70.00	15.00
10/5	Vou	111	111	11	45.00	960.00	(50.00)	20.00	20.00
10/7	Vou	112	112	9	20.00	980.00	(20.00)	-0-	20.00
10/21	PO	12		12			20.00	20.00	-0-
11/3	Vou	113	113	12	20.00	1,000.00	(20.00)	-0-	-0-
11/5	CrM	10361		8	(40.00)	960.00	-0-	-0-	40.00
11/17	PO	13		13			40.00	40.00	-0-
12/5	Vou	114	114	13	40.00	1,000.00	(40.00)	-0-	-0-

On July 1, four purchase orders were placed which encumbered $100, $50, $30, and $200. A running total of the encumbrances is kept in the Encumbered-Year-to-Date column and the same amounts are subtracted from the beginning balance, so that you always know the amount you have to work with.

Sometime between July 1 and July 6, three shipments of materials arrived, were verified, invoices were signed, and vouchers were prepared. Voucher 101 refers back to PO 1. Of the original $100 order, $50 worth of materials arrived and were paid for. Therefore, you need to add $50 to the Expended column and subtract $50 from both the Encumbered column and the running total of encumbrances. Because the $50 had already been taken from the Present Balance on July 1, that column does not change.

Voucher 102 refers back to PO 2, a $50 order. The entire order was received and $50 was paid and noted in the Expended column. The Expended-Year-to-Date column is increased by $50, and both the Encumbered and the Encumbered-Year-to-Date columns are decreased by $50. The Present Balance remains the same.

Voucher 103 refers back to PO 4, an order for $200 worth of materials. In this case, the order was complete but there was a 5 percent discount, and the cost, $190, is noted in the Expended column and added to the Expended-Year-to-Date column. The original encumbrance, $200, is subtracted from the Encumbered- Year-to-Date column. Since you recovered $10 on the order, you add $10 to the Present Balance. You now have $630, rather than $620, to spend. To continue the ledger, see the following possibilities.

On July 7 and 8, two more purchase orders were placed, for $130 worth of materials. As of July 8, you encumbered $210 and have a balance of $500 to spend.

On July 9, voucher 103.5, which refers back to PO 1, is paid. One of the ordered books is out of print; so the remainder of the order has been filled at a cost of $40, $10 less than anticipated. The Expended-Year-to-Date column is increased by $40; the encumbrance of $50 is subtracted from both the Encumbered and Encumbered-Year-to-Date columns. Because you have recovered $10, you add it to the Present Balance.

The next unusual occurrence is the payment of Voucher 104. If you refer back to PO 6, you see that $100 had been encumbered, but a price increase brought the actual expenditure to $110, which is added to the Expended-Year-to-Date running total. Since you had encumbered $100, you subtract that amount from the Encumbered column, but you add the full $110 to the Encumbered-Year-to-Date column. Since you spent $10 more than planned, you subtract $10 from the Present Balance.

No significant action occurs again until November 5, when a credit memo arrives and refers to PO 8. You are receiving a credit for $40; therefore you subtract $40 from both the Expended and the Expended-Year-to-Date columns. This adds nothing to either of the encumbrance columns, and it brings your present balance to $40. It allows you to issue PO 13, which is accomplished through Voucher 114 on December 5, and your Expended-Year-to-Date column is brought to $1,000, your beginning balance as of July 1.

You usually receive monthly accounting sheets that provide the breakdown of the various fund accounts and actions during that month. Normally, this is the formal organizational version of the encumbrance journal that you have been keeping. (It will therefore look somewhat familiar.) An example of such a report is presented in figure 36.

Your major function is to verify that the various expenditures and encumbrances were authorized and that books, materials, and services have actually been rendered or received, before payment is made. If a payment has been made for something you have not received, it is an error and should be speedily reported as such to the accounting office. If, on the other hand, an item has been received and payment has not been made within 30 to 90 days, you can assist your parent organization by calling it to the attention of the accounting office. One of your functions is to work with suppliers and keep their good will by seeing that they are paid as soon as possible after their goods or services have been provided. In effect, you have learned to interpret these reports by maintaining your *own* encumbrance journal.

Some accounting reports may provide analyses, such as percent of expenditures and/or encumbrances. Generally, they should match or parallel the amounts for the completed budget year. For instance, at the close of the first quarter, about one-fourth of the personnel, contract services, and utilities items should have been expended. Utilities might be a smaller percentage if the cooling system is less costly to operate than the heating system, but in general each item can readily be indexed against the amount for the past year. This is a quick check and should be made routinely for each account for which you are responsible. It makes it possible for you to identify accounts that are ahead of or behind your expectations on expenditures. If you are overexpended, you must devise a method of slowing expenditures for the next period, or risk being overexpended at the end of the budget year. If you are underexpended, you can increase expenditures, if there is need for the items in that budget category.

Other accounts (supplies, materials, and equipment) may be expended unevenly during the year. For instance, you may need to stock up on or purchase large amounts of items early in the year, or take advantage of price reductions for bulk purchases. This would place an additional burden on the supply line item early in the budget year, but will be balanced through smaller expenditures later. Equipment is usually ordered early to provide time for vendors to process the orders and deliver the equipment by midyear. This would give the equipment account a large encumbrance, followed by a long period of inaction (during which the vendors order and receive that equipment), and then a large expenditure when the equipment is received at the library and payment authorized.

As in all situations, practices differ. You must become well versed in the accounting procedures of your parent organization. The best way is to go to the accounting office and request training in these details early in your career. When there are questions or issues you do not understand, ask for assistance. This enhances your stature in the eyes of management and provides you with the skills to carry out your responsibilities as library manager.

PERSONNEL RELEASED FUNDS

During a typical year, some of your staff will take leave without pay (LWOP); some will resign, leaving their positions vacant; some will work fewer hours than scheduled; some will work overtime. Vacancies will often be filled at either a lower or higher rate of pay. All of these situations will affect your personnel budget; so you need to know where that budget stands. Figure 37 suggests a method for tracking use of these funds.

Use one card per position, as illustrated. On October 1 the reference librarian resigned, and since it took three months to fill the position, you recovered $1,167 each month. (Because the Recovered column is a running total, your Balance remained the same during the months the position was vacant.)

On January 1 you hire an experienced librarian and agree to pay an annual salary of $17,004. Note the name of the replacement and the new salary rate.

Pay Date	Amt. Paid	Encumbered	Recovered	Balance
1/1 Kate Smith, annual salary, $17,004.				

If you are reasonably certain that Kate will be with you the rest of the fiscal year, calculate the difference between the monthly pay for Joan and Kate ($250) and multiply it by the number of pay periods left (6), to arrive at $1,500. This means you will be spending $1,500 more on this position than you had budgeted, so enter that information into the Encumbered column, as shown in figure 38.

During the month of April, Kate took LWOP; therefore $1,417 was added to the Recovered column. By the end of the fiscal year, the Balance is $3,418, which should equal the sums in the Encumbered and the Recovered columns.

Figure 36. Monthly Printout of Expenditures

```
30-DEC-93 14:05:51              Albuquerque T-VI (PROD)
FISCAL YEAR 94                  Organization Detail Activity
                               From 01-OCT-93 To 30-NOV-93


COAS: 1              Alb Technical Vocational Institute
ORG: 1101           Main Library

TRANS     TRAN    DOCUMENT  DOCUMENT
DATE      TYPE    NUMBER    REF #        DESCRIPTION

                            Operating

11/29/93 INEI   I0021796            COMPUTERLAND OF ALBUQUERQUE
11/30/93 JE15   J0001253            Central Stores November 1993
11/30/93 JE15   J0001273            BOOKSTORE NOVEMBER 1993
ENDING BALANCE:           Supplies


BEGINNING BALANCE:   Travel
ENDING BALANCE:      Travel


BEGINNING BALANCE:   Shipping & Receiving
ENDING BALANCE:      Shipping & Receiving


BEGINNING BALANCE:   Allocated Data Processing
ENDING BALANCE:      Allocated Data Processing


BEGINNING BALANCE:   Printing Duplicating & Postal
ENDING BALANCE:      Printing Duplicating & Postal


BEGINNING BALANCE:   Telephone
10/11/93 JE15   J0001058            Phone-Main Library
ENDING BALANCE:      Telephone


BEGINNING BALANCE:   Equipment
10/15/93 PORD   PP136626            ACTRONICS
10/19/93 INEI   I0021110            NEWSBANK INC
10/19/93 INEI   I0021110            NEWSBANK INC
10/22/93 BD03   J9000223            update newsbank computer hardw
10/26/93 BD03   J9000226            To complete circulation sys in
11/04/93 PORD   PP136835            NEWSBANK INC
ENDING BALANCE:      Equipment


BEGINNING BALANCE:   Libarary Books
10/01/93 INEI   I0018866            DUN & BRADSTREET
10/01/93 INEI   I0018866            DUN & BRADSTREET
10/01/93 INEI   I0020304            LEARNING RESOURCES ASSOC
10/01/93 INEI   I0020304            LEARNING RESOURCES ASSOC
10/01/93 INEI   I0020929            LAWYERS COOPERATIVE PUBLISHING
10/01/93 INEI   I0020929            LAWYERS COOPERATIVE PUBLISHING
10/05/93 PORD   PP136461            EBSCO SUBSCRIPTION SERVICES
10/05/93 PORD   PP136492            LIBRARY CORPORATION
10/06/93 CNEI   00110934 I0018209   MATTHEW BENDER & COMPANY INC
```

PAGE 229
FGRODTA

ACCOUNT/ FUND	BUDGET ACTIVITY	TRANSACTION ACTIVITY	ENCUMBRANCE ACTIVITY	CMT TYP
1001				
8202			-189.00	U
8202		86.98		U
8202		253.04		U
8202	33,003.00	11,859.49	1,542.35	
8203	1,100.00	.00	.00	
8203	1,100.00	.00	.00	
8220	7,891.00	.00	.00	
8220	7,891.00	.00	.00	
8221	13,925.00	.00	.00	
8221	13,925.00	.00	.00	
8222	3,825.00	351.64	.00	
8222	3,825.00	351.64	.00	
8227	1,936.00	.00	.00	
8227		190.70		
8227	1,936.00	190.70	.00	
8304	10,000.00	1,216.85	6,626.65	
8304			10,000.00	U
8304		447.50		U
8304			-447.50	U
8304	800.00			
8304	2,412.00			
8304			800.00	
8304	13,212.00	1,664.35	16,979.15	
8306	142,357.00	76,605.72	-13,745.50	
8306		946.50		
8306			-946.50	
8306		48.00		
8306			-48.00	
8306		43.25		U
8306			-43.25	U
8306			43.88	
8306			1,690.00	
8306		-74.17		

Figure 37. Personnel Released-Funds Record

Acct. #110			Budgeted	$14,004
Name Joan Brown		Position Ref. Librn.	Pay Period	Monthly
Budget Reference Page 1, line 1				
Pay Date	Amt. Paid	Encumbered	Recovered	Balance
7/1				$14,004
7/31	$1,167	$1,167	-0-	12,837
8/31	1,167	2,334	-0-	11,670
9/31	1,167	3,501	-0-	10,503
10/31	-0-	3,501	$1,167	10,503
11/31	-0-	3,501	2,334	10,503
12/31	-0-	3,501	3,501	10,503

Figure 38. Personnel Released Funds (showing personnel change)

Pay Date	Amt. Paid	Encumbered	Recovered	Balance
1/31	$1,417	($1,500)	$3,501	$9,086
2/28	1,417	(1,500)	3,501	7,669
3/31	1,417	(1,500)	3,501	6,252
4/31	-0-	(1,500)	4,918	6,252
5/31	1,417	(1,500)	4,918	4,835
6/31	1,417	(1,500)	4,918	3,418

Since each card is limited to the salary for one position, you need a summary of the cards for decision making. Create a worksheet, which is kept in pencil so you can erase and rewrite, and include the following information:

Name	Position	Budgeted Amount	Actual Pay	$ Gained (Lost)	Total

The worksheet will probably be most useful if the names and positions are entered in the order they appear on your budget document. This offers a double check on accuracy. Entries into the worksheet should be made from the cards at the end of every pay period. They will be dated entries, instead of a running commentary, because each line is brought up to date by erasing old information and replacing it with new. This is not as messy as it sounds, because most of your staff will experience no changes during the year.

As of 9/31, for example, information from Joan Brown's card will read as follows:

Name	Position	Budgeted Amount	Actual Pay	$ Gained (Lost)	Total
Brown, J.	Ref. Librn.	$14,004	$3,501		

On 1/31, Joan Brown's name will be erased and replaced with Kate Smith's, and Actual Pay will be adjusted to reflect an additional $1,417. The amount of money gained during the months the position was vacant will be entered into the $ Gained (Lost) column. The column total will reflect that amount of gain, $3,501, and the worksheet will look like this:

Name	Position	Budgeted Amount	Actual Pay	$ Gained (Lost)	Total
Smith, K.	Ref. Librn.	$14,004	$4,918	$3,501	$3,501

At the end of April, the worksheet entry will be changed to reflect the LWOP:

Name	Position	Budgeted Amount	Actual Pay	$ Gained (Lost)	Total
Smith, K.	Ref. Librn.	$14,004	$7,752	$4,918	$4,918

At any time, you can add up the Total column to find out how much money you have recovered or overspent. After you have kept records like these for a few years, you will be able to predict, at the beginning of each year, how much of your budget you are likely to recover. You can use this prediction to make staffing, hiring, and salary decisions throughout the year or you can use a spreadsheet program on your PC, create your own system and manage it through the PC (see Chapter 12).

As you can observe, these records provide you with up-to-date information regarding your budget line items. For instance, if your parent organization comes through with a recision demand for your budget, you will have the information at hand that will assist you in determining if you already have funds in the personnel account lines to cover this recision amount. This knowledge will prevent a panic response to such a demand. Even if you have to make personnel cutbacks to meet the recisionary demand, you have the data and salary history to assist you in making the best of a negative situation.

As in the example above, you have identified an "extra" $4,918 in your personnel line item due to changes during the year in the reference librarian position. This money could be used to meet nearly all of a $5,000 recision demand, or half of a $10,000 recision figure. As recision demands get larger, the function budget analysis developed in Chapter 4 becomes the basis of your focus. The initial determination of the priorities for various services would be reviewed and those of the lowest rank modified or eliminated until sufficient funds had been retrieved to meet the recision amount.

PETTY CASH VOUCHER

Although most of your expenditures will be made by check, there will be occasions when you will have to use small amounts of cash, and it is for these occasions that a petty cash fund is established. You (or your accountant) will estimate the amount needed for a month, a check will be cashed for that amount, and the money placed in a secure petty cash box. To control disbursements from that supply of cash, you can use a form called a *petty cash voucher,* which might look like figure 39.

Figure 39. Petty Cash Voucher

Petty Cash Voucher	
	No. _____
	Date _____
Pay to _____ Amount _____	
For _____	
Approved by	Payment Received
_____	_____

At the end of each day, the money in the petty cash box and all the vouchers must add up to the beginning balance. In other words, the balance with which the fund began, minus the voucher totals, must equal the cash on hand. After a purchase with petty cash, the supplier must give you the receipt. These receipts are matched with their vouchers and all are batched together according to account. They are then entered into a petty cash book (figure 40).

Figure 40. Petty Cash Book

Date	Explanation	Vou. #	Receipts	Payments	Ofc. Sup.	Post.	Other Items	
1992							Items	Amt.
July 1	Check #54	Cashed	50.00					
3	Stamps	1		20.00		20.00		
7	Pamphlet	2		.50			pam.	.50
9	Pens	3		4.50	4.50			
14	Pencils	4		2.75	2.75			
			50.00	27.75	7.25	20.00		.50
15	Balance		22.25					

To replenish the petty cash fund, obtain and cash a check from your accounting office for the $27.75 that has been expended. All payments from petty cash will be charged to the appropriate accounts, at the time the check is drawn to reimburse the petty cash fund.

EQUIPMENT

Equipment orders almost always present problems, due either to untimely delivery or delivery of damaged goods. It is recommended that once your equipment budget is approved, you order the items immediately. It is not unusual to wait six months for delivery, and if a piece arrives damaged, you need time to make a claim and receive a replacement.

If you wait until January or February to order and the goods have not arrived before June 30, you will not have expended the appropriated amount. It will be returned to the general fund and may or may not be reappropriated the following year. Therefore, order equipment early in the year and be diligent in working with suppliers to assure that such equipment is received before the end of the fiscal year.

REPLACEMENT SCHEDULE

If you create a replacement schedule for each piece of equipment as it is received, budgeting for replacements will be infinitely easier in the future. First, estimate the useful life of the equipment. The vendor will give you an estimated lifespan, but alter that estimate to reflect use in your library. For example, if the vendor tells you a microfilm reader has a life of so many hours, use your data on your equipment and furniture and convert the hourly use into years. The replacement schedule can be kept on 3-by-5 cards that identify equipment by inventory number, vendor, date of purchase, and cost. The cards should be filed by date of replacement. This is another place where a PC record system would be valuable. Information stored in such files act as an immediate prompter when you are working on your budget preparation activities.

When a recision demand is made, if you have some unencumbered equipment money, you may determine that part or all of those funds represent the least harmful source to meet the recision. Remember to review your equipment replacement schedule before taking final action. Also look at the way your equipment is actually functioning. Sometimes it is possible to deter replacement and rebudget that equipment for the following year. These funds could then be used to help with the recision.

You can look in your collection of data each year, when you prepare your budget, to find items that should be replaced. If, after examining the furniture or equipment, you think its replacement can be postponed, you can change the replacement date and file the information again.

Using basic bookkeeping systems, you can control and account for your fund expenditures at any time during the fiscal year. Your goal is neither to overspend nor underspend your budget. To do this requires constant vigilance, but you will be rewarded by gaining the reputation of a good manager.

PRACTICE EXPERIENCES

1. On a PC, set up a ledger file for at least one line item.

2. Identify five pieces of equipment and prepare a replacement schedule for them.

3. Describe a petty cash voucher.

4. Differentiate between a requistion and a purchase order. What are the reasons that they are often combined on one form?

5. Summarize the reasons why you want to know about personnel expenditures.

SELECTED READINGS

Bennett, Paul. *Up Your Accountability.* Washington, D.C.: Taft Products, 1993.

Gambino, Anthony J., and Thomas J. Reardon. *Financial Planning and Evaluation for the Nonprofit Organization.* New York: National Association of Accountants, 1981.

Gross, Malvern J., and William Warshauer. *Financial and Accounting Guide for Nonprofit Organizations.* Rev. 2nd ed. New York: Wiley, 1983.

Powell, Ray M. *Budgetary Control Procedures for Institutions.* Notre Dame, Ind.: Univ. of Notre Dame Pr., 1980.

Razek, Joseph R. *Introduction to Governmental and Not-for-Profit Accounting.* Englewood Cliffs, NJ: Prentice-Hall, 1990.

12
Automating the Budget

This chapter offers suggestions for placing your library budget on a PC. In the past this was a tedious and time consuming task requiring complicated computer commands, however, today's computer world eases the pain and time requirements. For instance, PCs using the 386 SX and 486 SX chips are designed to use programs like Windows and WYSIWYG (What You See Is What You Get) to simplify your computing life and speed up all your computer processes. The Lotus 1-2-3 computer language is available and instructions come with the language purchase packages. Often these packages are included in computer purchases. So if you have tried to put your budget on a computer before and given up, it's time to try again.

In this chapter, you will find suggested formats for parts of your budget. All of these examples were produced on PCs using Lotus 1-2-3, some brand of Windows and WYSIWYG. These formats are suggestions. As you learn to use your PC for budget accounting, you will find many other uses that may simplify your life (like development of report formats) and help you become more effective as a library manager.

This chapter will not teach you how to use Lotus or any other program, but suggestions will be made to help you with decisions about such programs and the equipment needed to support them. To support the demands, the following parameters are recommended:

> A PC equal to a BSR 486 SX (or 386 SX) with a 2 megabyte RAM (get 4, if you can); 80–120+ megabyte hard drive; 32k memory cache; high density floppy disk drive. Ask for:
> A .31 dot-pitch monitor (much easier on the eyes and definitive) and a color disc video card with 512k, VRAM.
> While a 486 SX is preferred, a 386 SX will do the job. Just remember that the Windows package uses lots of space and you

do not want to be limited as you develop your file formats and enter your files.

PROGRAMS NEEDED

As mentioned, get Lotus Development Corporation 1-2-3, a Windows package (like Windows 3.1), a WYSIWYG package, or Borland International Inc., Quatro Pro for Windows, or Microsoft's Excel Word for Windows (Dolonas, p.70).

The overall budget layout might follow the structure that you find in figure 41. This is produced on Lotus 1-2-3 with Windows. It is simple to create using Windows and through that program many of the intricate commands can be avoided, making your computer work easier and faster. Most users today also make use of a WYSIWYG program. This concept of "what you see is what you get," lets you choose through boxing or highlighting the sections of any of the charts that you have created and want to print. Additionally, you actually see what the chart, figure or graphics will look like on the printed page.

Most of these computers and programs depend on the use of a "mouse" that lets you choose which segment of the file you wish to work on, move or manipulate in some way.

One of the best publications in this area is still the *Essential Guide to the Library IBM PC*, produced in the late 1980s by Meckler Corporation. Its thirteen volumes answer almost any question. Of course, additional books have been produced since then. It would be wise to get into a training session that would make you operational in Lotus 1-2-3 with Windows, Excel or Quatro Pro. This gives you the flexibility to deal with your own needs without a slavish adherence to extensive programming commands. Once you get the hang of it, it is interesting and exciting to develop your own file formats and structures that meet your needs.

Updating of files is also simpler and faster if you use Windows. You see what you are adding, changing or deleting and how it fits into the overall patterns of your file as you work on your entries.

The advantage of using the more contemporary state-of-the-art (circa 1993) programs and equipment is that you do not have to get lost in extensive programming command codes that were previously required to establish the formats and reports you want to create.

To develop the necessary file formats for your needs you might find an intern from a nearby university or community college to do the development work for your library on, or for your PC. Look for students in the data processing program, an accounting program or a management program. Often it is possible for them to obtain credit hours for an internship, a problems course, or as part of a project team providing community agency service with a technical outcome (the production of your programs). If you have this opportunity, also request that a training program be included to train you and some of your significant staff on the programs using your own equipment. Your contact person is usually a department chairperson. Commmunity colleges are often the most responsive to such requests. Occasionally, a class project is developed and a number of students work with you to produce the programs desired. You must define what you want and also the equipment parameters of your hardware and software.

AREAS FOR PROGRAM DEVELOPMENT

The most productive areas for program development are:

> A line-item budget for the year, with columns for keeping track of requisitions and total encumbrances to date for each line item, and a running balance for each (so you can be current with daily or weekly updates).
> A requisition/purchase order file to include order numbers, dates of orders, changes in orders, and the National Institute of Government Procurement (NIGP) Commodity Service Code Number.

To set up an overall budget file, you can follow the format in figure 41. This particular figure represents the conditions of the accounts with approximately one month of the budget remaining in the fiscal year. The line items are in the column along the left hand margin, each described with its line-item number and title for that line item. The first column across the top indicates the adjusted budget balance for each line item. It is titled "adjusted" because it represents the amount approved for the budget, plus or minus any additions or recisions that have occurred during the operational year. The next column is the "Expended to Date" column. This is the summary that you adjust from your individual line-item files on a daily, weekly, or monthly basis. The rule of thumb is to adjust this amount as often as you can, so that the overall status of the budget line is as current as possible. Of course, these are always posted and brought up to date before any reports are printed, either for the staff or the upper management. The "remaining balance" is the difference between the adjusted balance and the amount "expended to date." This tells you and anyone else at a glance where you stand and allows you to report accurately where you are for each line at any time.

The final column in this format is for comparison only. Your business office generally will provide you with a monthly summary in which they show the status on each line item according to their information. You can expect this to differ from your own figures, because yours are more current. You have immediate knowledge concerning changes in purchase orders or shipping costs. You will then be able to inform them as to why the differences exist as well as report these reasons in the required reports to your parent organization. Sometimes the differences are due to posting procedure differences, sometimes they reflect mistakes that either you or the business office made in entering figures into the file, while sometimes they are the result of the timing of posting items to the file. Usually you will be more current than the business office because you get the information sooner than they do. Such a column is valuable in order to communicate as effectively as possible with your business office contact person. Usually, this column is not put on reports for your staff due to its confusion impact. Others may not be as informed as you are with regard to what these apparent differences mean and why they exist.

For instance, look at Library Books (8306). Notice that the difference between your records and those of the business office is substantial. You have brought your file up to date, since you want to expend as much as possible in this final period. The business office still is not as current as you are. This is the time to confer with the business office to bring them up to date so they do not disallow any of your final book purchase orders. Figure 42 represents another budget that was prepared with Lotus 1-2-3 using Windows. As you will notice, the same system is used and the product is similar.

Figure 43 is a subsystem file for a particular publisher and contains information that allows the user to move into the summary files for reports. Here you will find the invoice numbers, dates of invoices, the amount of the invoices, amounts representing revisions to the invoice, and the current balance. The system used by this organization has a "blanket" purchase order amount that is assigned to this publisher at the beginning of the year. Throughout the year, as the invoices are cut to that publisher, the amounts are subtracted from that balance.

Also, notice that as revisions were made, they added back into the account balance. In this way the file is kept accurate on a routine basis.

Figure 44 is from a file that keeps track of the invoices as they are issued. This is very much like the old account ledger that was kept manually before the advent of PC accounting. The first column is date, the second, vendor, the third is the NIGP Commodity/Service Code Number that is now required on all items ordered by governmental entities. The fourth column is the requisition number under which the order was submitted or the activity took place. The fifth column is the amount of the requisition, with the next column for revisions to the

Figure 41. Overall Budget Layout: Library Services Combined Budget Summary

Library Services Budget Fiscal 1992–1993				
Main Library				
Account #1001 1101 XXX 111	Adjusted	Expended	Remaining	Bus. Off
	Balance	to Date	Balance	Balance
8010 Aides Full-Time	0.00	0.00	0.00	0.00
8011 Aides Part-Time	0.00	0.00	0.00	0.00
8012 Aides Substitute	0.00	0.00	0.00	0.00
8013 Aides Overtime	0.00	0.00	0.00	0.00
8020 Professional Full-Time	108,918.00	99,223.00	9,695.00	0.00
8021 Professional Part-Time	0.00	0.00	0.00	0.00
8030 Clerical Full-Time	145,686.00	143,724.00	1,962.00	0.00
8031 Clerical Part-Time	0.00	0.00	0.00	0.00
8032 Clerical Overtime	0.00	0.00	0.00	0.00
8061 Work Study-State Match	11,732.00	9,893.00	1,839.00	0.00
8063 Work Study-Federal Match	3,187.00	2,636.00	551.00	0.00
8063 Work Study-TVI	39,312.00	39,312.00	0.00	0.00
8201 Contract Services	8,190.00	8,190.00	0.00	0.00
8202 Supplies	32,198.00	33,003.00	(805.00)	0.00
8203 Travel	1,100.00	1,100.00	0.00	0.00
8219 Motor Pool	0.00	0.00	0.00	0.00
8220 Shipping Receiving	3,968.00	3,968.00	0.00	0.00
8221 Allocated Data Processing	12,456.00	12,456.00	0.00	0.00
8222 Printing Duplicating & Postal	1,233.00	1,233.00	0.00	0.00
8227 Telephone	1,935.00	1,935.00	0.00	0.00
8304 Equipment	13,278.00	0.00	13,278.00	0.00
8306 Library Books	201,294.00	231,100.00	(29,806.00)	0.00
Total Library Services Budget	—	—	(3,286.00)	0.00
Total Blanket Funds Remaining	584,487.00	587,773.00	0.00	
Gross Budget Remaining	584,487.00	587,773.00	(3,286.00)	0.00
Percentage Sub-Totals		100.56%	−0.56%	

Audiovisual Services				
Main & Montoya Combined				
Account #1001 1201 XXXX 112	Adjusted	Expended	Remaining	Bus. Off
	Balance	to Date	Balance	Balance
8010 Aides Full-Time	0.00	0.00	0.00	0.00
8011 Aides Part-Time	0.00	0.00	0.00	0.00
8012 Aides Substitute	0.00	0.00	0.00	0.00
8013 Aides Overtime	0.00	0.00	0.00	0.00
8020 Professional Full-Time			0.00	0.00
8021 Professional Part-Time	0.00	0.00	0.00	0.00
8030 Clerical Full-Time	94,274.00	94,274.00	0.00	0.00
8031 Clerical Part-Time	0.00	0.00	0.00	0.00
8032 Clerical Overtime	0.00	0.00	0.00	0.00
8061 Work Study-State Match	4,025.00	4,025.00	0.00	0.00
8063 Work Study-Federal Match	680.00	680.00	0.00	0.00
8063 Work Study-TVI	15,027.00	15,027.00	0.00	0.00
8201 Contract Services	3,320.00	3,320.00	0.00	0.00
8202 Supplies	9,160.00	9,160.00	0.00	0.00
8203 Travel			0.00	0.00
8219 Motor Pool	0.00	0.00	0.00	0.00
8220 Shipping Receiving	2,345.00	2,345.00	0.00	0.00
8221 Allocated Data Processing	0.00	0.00	0.00	0.00
8222 Printing Duplicating & Postal	230.00	230.00	0.00	0.00
8227 Telephone	1,122.00	1,122.00	0.00	0.00
8304 Equipment	0.00	0.00	0.00	0.00
8306 Library Books	21,033.31	21,033.31	0.00	0.00
Totals	130,183.00	130,183.00	0.00	0.00
Percentage of Budget Remaining		100.00%	0.00%	

Figure 42. Budget Format Using Lotus 1-2-3: Main Library Summary Sample

Library Services Budget Fiscal 1992–1993					
Main Campus Library Budget Summary - 1001 1101 XXXX 111					
	Adjusted	Start	Expended	Revisions	Remaining
	Balances	Balances	to Date		Balance
8010 Aides Full-Time					0.00
8011 Aides Part-Time					0.00
8012 Aides Substitute					0.00
8013 Aides Overtime					0.00
8020 Professional Full-Time	108,918.00	99,223.00	95,759.00	0.00	3,464.00
8021 Professional Part-Time					0.00
8030 Clerical Full-Time	145,686.00	143,724.00	102,000.00	1,532.00	43,256.00
8031 Clerical Part-Time			0.00	0.00	0.00
8032 Clerical Overtime					0.00
8061 Work Study-State Match	11,732.00	9,893.00	14,256.25	3,000.00	(1,363.25)
8063 Work Study-Federal Match	3,187.00	2,636.00	1,845.00	0.00	791.00
8063 Work Study-TVI	39,312.00	39,312.00	37,589.00	0.00	1,723.00
8201 Contract Services	8,190.00	8,190.00	11,325.00	0.00	(3,135.00)
8202 Supplies	32,198.00	33,003.00	24,156.00	0.00	8,847.00
8203 Travel	1,100.00	1,100.00	2,458.00	0.00	(1,358.00)
8220 Shipping Receiving	3,968.00	3,968.00	0.00	0.00	3,968.00
8221 Allocated Data Processing	12,456.00	12,456.00	1,500.00		10,956.00
8222 Printing Duplicating	1,233.00	1,233.00	842.00	0.00	391.00
8227 Telephone	1,935.00	1,935.00	0.00	0.00	1,935.00
8304 Equipment	13,278.00		13,500.00	0.00	(13,500.00)
8306 Library Books	201,294.00	231,100.00	210,000.00	0.00	21,100.00
Total Library Services Budget	584,487.00	587,773.00	515,230.25	4,532.00	77,074.75
Percentage Sub-Totals			0.88	0.01	0.13

requisition. Finally, there is the column that keeps the running balance for this line item.

These four files can track your accounts and provide you with accurate and up-to-date information. They can help you prepare budget reports accurately and easily. As you work with the programs introduced in this chapter, you will find yourself creating others that can contribute to your skills and stature as an effective library manager.

Figure 43. File Subsystem: Blanket Requisitions Sample

Quality Books		Invoice Number	Date	Amount	Revision	Current Balance
Main						
						5,000.00
		317023	08/14/92	229.29		4,770.71
		317014	08/14/92	3667.76		1,102.95
		317827	08/27/92	15.81		1,087.14
		318571	09/10/92	12.84		1,074.30
		CM318647	09/10/92		−36	1,110.30
		CM320118	09/28/92		−67.6	1,177.90
		330966	02/02/93	1706.98		(529.08)
Rev. Typed		Closed	03/30/93		−529.08	0.00
						0.00

Figure 44. Invoice Ledger: Book Account Sample

		Account # 8306 Library Books					
Date	Vendor	Commidity Code	Number	Invoice Amount	P.O. #.	Revis.	Remaining Balance
07/01/92	Start Balance:						180000.00
07/14/92	UNM Press	705	758573	9.57			179990.43
07/14/92	Dun & Bradstreet	705	7077092	811.5			179178.93
07/14/92	Ingram	705	22501829	168.07			179010.86
07/14/92	Midwest	705	2754166	8206.64			170804.22
07/14/92	Alb. Journal	906	REN. ATT.	57			170747.22
07/14/92	RIA	896	REN. ATT.	275			170472.22
07/14/92	U. of Texas	705	333901	9.88	130894		170462.34
07/14/92	Warren, Gorham, Lamont	705	4385720	84.95			170377.39
07/14/92	A M Best	705	REN. ATT.	150			170227.39
07/14/92	Alb. Publishing	705	FOR PUR.	5.25	130850		170222.14
07/14/92	UNM	705	FOR PUR.	26.5	130868		170195.64
07/14/92	High Impact	705	FOR PUR.	15.15	130916		170180.49
07/14/92	Northwest Reg. Educ. Lab	705	FOR PUR.	14.8	130917		170165.69
07/14/92	Bowker	705	FOR PUR.	213.41	130849		169952.28
07/14/92	Uswest	705	77938402	63.85			169888.43
07/14/92	Michie	705	9087	214.28			169674.15

PRACTICE EXPERIENCES

1. Develop a line-item budget format on a PC.
2. Enroll in a class to learn Lotus 1-2-3.
3. Identify the strengths and weaknesses of at least two Windows packages.
4. Describe the use of WYSIWYG.
5. What is a "mouse," and how does it work?
6. Obtain data on and compare at least two contemporary PCs.

SELECTED READINGS

Bonner, Paul. "Windows Development Tool Kit." *PC-Computing*. Vol. 4, November '92 p.290(10).

Coursey, David. "Lotus Gives Away Prewritten Programs." *InfoWorld*. Vol. 14, il., May 11 '92 p.33(2). (Lotus Development Corp. Lotus Notes Application Library.)

Dolonas, Michoios. "Spreadsheets Under Scrutiny." *Byte*. Nov. 15, 1992.

Dover, Marilyn. "Issues in the Use of Library Automation." *Computers in Libraries*. Vol. 12, April '92.

Ferkso-Weiss, Henry. "Streamline Your Simple Projects." *Personal Computing*. November, 1986.

Hayes, Sherman and Donald Brown. "Creative Budgeting and Funding for Automation: Getting the Goods!." *Wilson Library Bulletin*. Vol. 55, il., April '92 p.42(4).

Hernon, Peter, and Charles R. McClure, editors. *Microcomputers for Library Decision Making*. Norwood, NJ: Ablex Press, 1986.

Ihnatko, Andy. "Let's Get Visual." *MacUser*. Vol. 8, il., April '92 p.213(4).

LaRue, James. "Micro Management." *Wilson Library Bulletin*. Vol. 55, June '92 p.97(3).

Lauriston, Robert, Steve Bass, Scott Dunn, Richard Scoville, George Campbell, Celeste Robinson, Richard Jantz, Judy Heim, and Brett Glass. "The Experts' Favorites." *PC World*. Vol. 10, July '92 p.207(10).

Matthews, Joseph R. "An Explosion in Micro-Based Systems." *Computers in Libraries*. Vol. 11, il., November '91 p.8(5).

Novins, Kate and Larry L. Learn. "Linked Systems: Issues and Opportunities." (Special Section: Report from the OCLC/RGL Seminar), *Information Technology and Libraries*. Vol. 10, June '91 p.155(6).

Glossary

activity Operations which are essential to the survival of the library.

approved budget The authorized expenditure, in budget categories, approved by the parent organization before the beginning of the budget year.

base package In zero base budgeting, the first-level package that addresses the most important activities performed by a decision unit.

block grant Money given with no line-item restrictions.

capital outlay Budget category for long-term expenditures, often over several years. Always includes costs for building construction or remodeling; often includes equipment.

categorical funds Funds granted for expenditures for specific purposes.

decision package Discrete sets of services, activities or expenditure items in a decision unit.

decision unit A program, function, organization unit, or line-item that is to be justified in a zero base budget.

encumbrance A claim made on a budget, before payment, for service rendered or item ordered.

formal organization The organization as it appears on a formal organization chart.

formative evaluation Assessment of the processes used during a project or program.

FTE Full-time equivalent of staff.

function budget A budget in which the various functions of the library are separately identified for the purposes of allocation of funds.

function The broadest organization subunits of the library.

Gantt chart A bar chart, showing the times of activities in a sequence.

guidelines Rule-of-thumb percentage limit of increase or decreases to be applied in the preparation of the next year's budget.

hard match Money given contingent on the recipient's guarantee to provide, in actual dollars, a certain amount of funding to a project.

increment Percentage to be applied to current budget to determine the subsequent budget.

indirect cost Proportion of a grant request for funds to be expended by an agency in administering a grant. Usually a fixed percentage of the grant amount. Also called overhead.

informal organization The organization as it functions.

ledger A book in which accounts are kept.

line-item budget The most common budget format, arranged with each category of expenditure identified on a separate line.

operating expenses Costs of operating the library, such as salaries, rent, heat, and utilities. Budgeted and expended on an annual basis.

PERT Program Evaluation Review Technique—a network system of charting.

petty cash Cash on hand to make small purchases.

price/cost indexing Constructing a scale to relate (index) increases in prices or costs to a previous "base" or cost.

program A subset of function. Group of closely related operations under which organizational activities and services can be clustered.

program budget Budget constructed so that program costs are separately identified.

purchase order Document to order goods or services.

purchase requisition Document to notify a buying agent (such as a controller) that goods and services are required.

recision Cutting the budget figures due to current or expected reductions in funding.

replacement schedule System used to predict dates when equipment and furniture will have to be replaced.

requisition purchase order Combined purchase requisition and purchase order.

revenue Income or appropriations.

services Operations which are optional to the survival of the library.

sort match or in-kind contributions Agency receiving a grant guarantees to provide a certain portion of resources in donated services, such as volunteer time, goods, and equipment.

summative evaluation Carried out at the end of a cycle of activities to determine accomplishment of objectives.

time-line chart Shows how activities or a project relate to each other in a time sequence.

voucher Documents authorizing payment.

zero base budgeting Planning technique requiring that costs of all functions, both current and new, be justified at the beginning of each budgetary cycle.

Index

155

Richard Rounds has been involved in libraries throughout his life as a user, developer, and administrator. For more than twenty years at the Albuquerque Technical-Vocational Institute, now a large community college, he worked with the library staff in the development of the library from its beginnings to the extensive contemporary library it is today. During these years he developed and used many of the budgeting concepts included in this work.